KOREAN FOOD 101:

A Glimpse into Everyday Dining

Korean Food 101: A Glimpse into Everyday Dining

First published in 2014
Fourth printing, 2019
by Hollym International Corp., Carlsbad, CA, USA
Phone 760 814 9880
http://www.hollym.com   **e-Mail** contact@hollym.com

⎰⎰ Hollym

Published simultaneously in Korea
by Hollym Corp., Publishers, Seoul, Korea
Phone +82 2 734 5087   **Fax** +82 2 730 5149
http://www.hollym.co.kr   **e-Mail** hollym@hollym.co.kr

ISBN: 978-1-56591-458-2
Library of Congress Control Number: 2014954183

Printed in Korea

KOREAN FOOD 101:

A Glimpse into Everyday Dining

by **KOREAN FOOD PROMOTION INSTITUTE**

Hollym

Carlsbad, CA and Seoul

PREFACE

The legendary Indian poet and Nobel laureate Rabindranath Tagore (1861-1941) once described Korea as "a bright light of the East." His intention was to highlight the splendid culture, as well as the national characteristics of creativity and courtesy.

The tradition of Korean food (*hansik*) developed over 5,000 years of human habitation in the Korean Peninsula, driven by a large variety of foods available over the four distinct seasons. This tradition embodies the cheerfulness and grace of the Korean people. The diverse types of *jang* (salted and fermented pastes or sauces) that makes up the core seasonings for preparing Korean food are healthy fermented foods created through a long period of fermentation, known in Korean as "*jangdokdae*" culture.

In his book *The Third Wave*, Alvin Toffler described the first flavor as salt, the second flavor as sauce, and projected that the third will be fermented food. In its March 2006 issue, the American monthly magazine *Health* designated kimchi, Korea's most famous fermented dish, as one of the world's five healthiest foods.

Korean Food 101: A Glimpse into Everyday Dining lists a selection of 101 Korean foods that we are proud to introduce to the world. This broad selection from the even vaster Korean menu explains the origination, taste, and functionality of each dish, along with Korean food culture in general. These representatives of Korean cuisine have been consumed by people from all walks of life, from the royal family to the general public, and are enjoyed today by K-pop stars, the main drivers of the Korean Wave, and contemporary Korean citizens.

I hope that this book will serve as an opportunity for people across the globe to develop a deeper understanding of Korean food culture.

Chairperson of the Korean Food Promotion Institute

CONTENTS

BAP & JUK
Cooked Grains and Porridge

014

042

062

086

110

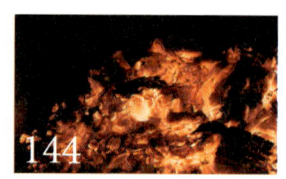
144

180

188

200

222

THE CULINARY CULTURE OF KOREA

All Dishes Served At Once

Korean meals, unlike western course meals, are served in a single setting. We call this *bansang charim*, where the rice (*bap*) and side dishes (*banchan*) are set together on the table. A *bansang* can be very simple, consisting of rice, soup, soy sauce, kimchi, grilled fish, and a vegetable dish. But it can also be extravagant with so many dishes spread out on the table that the table legs figuratively "bend." Regardless of the scale, the key point is that the combination is balanced and harmonious in terms of taste and nutrition.

Korean cuisine certainly does not lack variety. There is such a vast range of cooking methods that one rarely sees the same cooking method used twice on a given ingredient. For starters, cooked rice has countless variations: *huin-bap* (white rice), *japgok-bap* (multi-grain rice), and *seokkeum bap* (rice mixed with vegetables or seafood). There are over 350 varieties of *jusik* (main starch dish), including *bap*, *juk* (rice porridge), *guksu* (noodles), *mandu* (dumpling), *tteok-guk* (sliced rice cake soup), and *sujebi* (hand-pulled dough soup). There are also over 1,500 varieties of *banchans* which account for more than half of all Korean dishes.

Fermented Foods for Flavor and Nutrition

Fermented foods are central to the Korean diet, including several well-known examples: kimchi, salted seafood (*jeotgal*), and fermented condiments such as soy sauce (*ganjang*), soybean paste (*doenjang)* and red chili paste (*gochujang*). Oftentimes, the phrase "a deep flavor" is used to describe many Korean dishes. The expression refers to the complex taste that comes from seasoning with sauces that takes years to ferment and mature. Kimchi, which has over 350 known variations depending on ingredients and taste, has recently gained international recognition as a great source of lactobacilli and dietary fiber. The same kimchi will undergo subtle changes in flavor and texture with the passing of the seasons.

Fermented condiments, including soy sauce, soybean paste, and red chili paste, not only provide flavor but also significant nutritional benefits. As they are made mainly from protein-rich soybeans, these fermented sauces add protein to the side dishes which mainly consist of grains and vegetables. Amino acids created in the breakdown of proteins add a subtle flavor that envelops the palate, while microorganisms from the fermented condiments improve health through their digestion regulating and anti-oxidant properties. All fermented condiments are "live foods" packed with enzymes. Kimchi is a well-known health food rich in fiber and lactobacilli which promote digestion and physiological well-being.

Using Local, Fresh, and Seasonal Ingredients

The natural conditions of the land—facing the sea on three sides and having four distinct seasons—provided Koreans with a large variety of ingredients. People could also harvest seasonal wild herbs and plants from the mountains and hills. Hence, Korea's culinary tradition evolved around the seasons: *patjuk* (red bean porridge) for the winter solstice; piping hot soups on the three dog days of summer; and *ogokbap* (five-grain rice) and *namul* (seasoned vegetables) to celebrate the first full moon of the year. The foods offered to our ancestral spirits on Lunar New Year or Chuseok (fall harvest festival), are also made using the freshest ingredients in season.

Korea's indigenous regional cuisines reflect the geographical and climatic characteristics of that region. Made from cooking methods which are exclusive to that region and inherited from ancient times, regional cuisines are an intangible cultural heritage of immense value. Seasonal customs, rites of passage, and regional foods that reflect local customs all account for the great diversity and variety of *hansik*.

Spices and Garnish for Taste, Aesthetics, and Nutrition

Korean cooking employs a variety of spices (*yangnyeom*) and garnishes (*gomyeong*). The principle of *Euisik-dongwon*—"food in the mouth becomes medicine in body"—was practiced by combining ingredients and adding spices. Chili, garlic, green onion, and ginger were used often not simply because of the flavor, but also because of the health benefits. Spices (*yangnyeom*) is 藥念 in Chinese characters: the first character means "medicine" and the second one means "in mind." The word indicates that when using various spices one must "keep in mind that spices can be medicine to the body."

Korean dishes are frequently topped with garnishes. The ingredients used as garnishes in *hansik* follow the principle of Five Cardinal Colors, which consist of white, black, green, red, and yellow. *Gujeolpan* (platter of nine delicacies) and *sinseollo* (royal hot pot) are composed of color blocks, while *japchae* (stir-fried glass noodles and vegetables) and *tangpyeong-chae* (mung bean jelly salad) mix the colors together. The multi-colored garnish and natural food colorings show the great care Koreans put into preparing food. Garnishes balance taste and color, and represent the principle of Five Cardinal Colors which correspond to the five cosmic elements.

Table Manners and Tableware

• Soup Bowl and Rice Bowl, Spoon and Chopsticks

In a traditional Korean table setting, the rice bowl is placed to the left and the soup bowl to the right. Both the spoon and chopsticks are to be used. The spoon is a useful utensil, since *hansik* includes hot soups and stews, and chopsticks are ideal for handling dishes made with chopped or sliced ingredients. It is proper to use the spoon for rice and soup, and chopsticks for side dishes. Everyone must wait until the eldest person at the table picks up his/her chopstick or spoon. The utensils also represent the balance of *yin* and *yang*: the round spoon symbolizes *yin* and the chopsticks *yang*.

• The Number of *Cheop*

The size of a traditional Korean meal is measured by the number of *cheop*. There are 3-cheop, 5-*cheop*, 7-*cheop*, 9-*cheop* tables, and a 12-*cheop* table (*surasang*) which was reserved for kings. *Cheop* actually refers to the vessel used for side dishes. The basic 3-*cheop* table serves a vegetable dish, a grilled dish, and pickled vegetables. Since the rice, soup, kimchi, potstew (*jjigae*), and sauces are not included in the count, even a simple 3-*cheop* table offers plenty of flavorful dishes.

• *Yugi* and *Onggi*

Yugi means brassware, sometimes called *notgeureut* in Korean. There is also *bangjja*, a type of brassware hand-shaped by hammering a molten blend of 80 percent copper and 20 percent tin. Anseong in Gyeonggi Province has long been famous for its *yugi*. Making quality brassware by order of high-ranking officials or *yangban* was called as *"mochum"* or *"machum."* Hence, came the expression *"anseong-machum"* which Koreans use to refer to a "perfect fit." *Onggi* are vessels made by coating earthenware with lye and firing it at a high temperature. An *onggi*'s surface has countless microscopic holes which allow the vessel to breathe and keep its content fresh. It is ideal for preserving fermented foods such as kimchi, soy sauce, soybean paste, and red chili paste. *Ttukbaegi* is an *onggi* stew pot that can go over direct fire, as it can withstand high temperatures and cools slowly.

• *Soban*

Soban refers to a low table. *Gaksang-charim* is typical of traditional Korean table settings, meaning that each person eats from his or her own personal *soban*. *Soban* is known by different names depending on the material or the shape of the legs: *goimok-ban* is made of zelkova wood; *haengja-ban* is made of ginkgo; *gaedari-soban* has curved legs like a dog (*gae* means dog and *dari* means leg); and *samjok-ban* stands on only three legs (*sam* means three and *jok* means foot). Also famous is the *tongyeong-ban* from Tongyeong, South Gyeongsang Province; the *naju-ban* made in Naju, South Jeolla Province; and the *haeju-ban* crafted in Haeju, Hwanghae Province.

BAP & JUK
[Cooked Grains and Porridge]

Bap (cooked grains) is an integral part of Korean life. Koreans often say, "We live on *bap*," or "*Bap* is the best medicine." We also ask "Have you had your *bap*?" as a friendly greeting. The word *bapsang* (rice table) refers to a meal in general. And *juk* (rice congee or porridge) is the first thing a baby is fed when weaning, and a warm bowl of *juk* is believed to be the best food for people who are feeling weak or under the weather.

The Korean Staple
Bap
[Cooked Rice]

Bap can be made entirely of white rice (*huin-bap*), but it can also be combined with other grains such as soy bean or red bean (*japgok-bap*), with vegetables such as potatoes or sweet potatoes (*chaeso-bap*), or with seafood such as oysters or mussels (*haemul-bap*). Heat control during cooking determines the taste of *bap*. Even if the rice is stale or lacking in quality, savvy Koreans know how to cook delicious *bap* by adjusting the cooking temperature.

The Meal Will Only Taste as Good as the *Bap*

Bap, or rice is *ban* (飯) in Chinese characters. It is also called by many names depending on the person eating it: *jinji* for the elderly; *sura* for royalty; and *me* or *jetme* for ancestral rites. The Korean meal is incomplete without *bap*. Koreans can have a meal without side dishes if the *bap* tastes good enough, but not the other way around, no matter how tasty the side dishes are. That is why the side dishes and rice are served all at once, unlike Western course meals. One might wonder how the different tastes can be appreciated this way, but the charm of Korean food lies in the fusion and harmony of different flavors on the palate.

Rice Prevents Adulthood Diseases

Rice is highly effective in preventing obesity, because while it is rich in carbohydrates and protein, it contains 33 percent less fat than wheat flour. Blood sugar levels spike after eating bread or potatoes, but rise only moderately after consuming rice. Rice also contains peptide, which suppresses hypertension, as well as powerful natural antioxidants such as vitamin E, folic acid and tocotrienol which slow down the aging of cells. The most common and fundamental Korean food is *huin-bap* (white rice), which is softer, more delicious and more digestible than any other type of *bap*. *Hyeonmi-bap* (brown rice), which is made from unpolished rice and thus contains even greater amounts of important nutrients, is also popular as a health food along with *japgok-bap* (nutrious grain rice) and *chaeso-bap* (rice with vegetables).

How to Cook Delicious *Bap*
Perfectly cooked rice is lustrous, soft and has a sweet aroma. People of the Qing Dynasty used to praise the flavor of Korean-style cooked rice, saying, "The fire should be weak and little water should be used to cook rice. Joseon people are experts at making well-cooked glossy rice." Perhaps it was due to the important role of rice that we can find many literatures of the Joseon period elaborating on the art of rice-cooking.

The Scrumptious Crust
Dolsot-bap
[Stone Pot Rice]

Dolsot-bap is rice cooked in a stone pot (*dolsot*) with chestnuts, ginkgo nuts, pine nuts, shiitake mushrooms, soybeans, and vegetables. Because it has to be served piping hot straight off the stove, *dolsot-bap* was only made for special guests or the patriarch of the family.

A Special Rice Dish for One

There are several theories about the origin of *dolsot-bap*. Some say that it was first cooked for dignitaries visiting the royal palace. Some believe that it was created when the Joseon royal family went to the Beopju Temple in Sokri Mountain for a Buddhist prayer ceremony, and the monks cooked rice with ingredients available in the mountains. Still others claim that talc stone pots (*gobdol-sot*) were used to cook rice ever since the Choi clan from Jangsu—an area famous for natural talc—offered talc stone pots as tribute to King Sukjong of Joseon Dynasty. In the royal palace, *bap* for the King and the Queen was cooked separately in small talc stone pots over hardwood charcoal. First, they made a charcoal fire in a large brass brazier, placed two flat iron rods across the brazier, set a talc stone pot on the rods, boiled water for some time, added the rice, and finally simmered it slowly until it was thoroughly cooked. This process guarantees a soft taste that literally melts in the mouth.

They served both *huin-bap* (white rice) and *pat-bap* (rice with red beans) to offer the King and Queen a choice, but only two servings were prepared for each. This illustrates how *dolsot-bap* was served only to the very privileged. These days, *dolsot-bap* has become popularized, and many restaurants serve *dolsot-bap* rather than regular *bap* in a bowl. It is said that famous *dolsot-bap* restaurants still had burgeoning businesses even during the economic downturn during the 1997 Asian financial crisis.

Getting to the Bottom

Dolsot-bap is a gastronomic experience where the best comes last. After removing the cooked rice, water is poured into the stone bowl. The thin layer of scorched rice (*nurungji*) is cooked in the water by the residual heat from the pot and becomes *sungnyung* (browned rice tea). By the time the meal is finished, the *sungnyung* is ready. *Dolsot-bap* enthusiasts claim that no meal is complete until they have washed it down with hot *nurungji* and some salted seafood or pickled vegetables. In order to make the best tasting *sungnyung*, the added ingredients should not leave any unpleasant odor. Thus, chestnuts, jujubes, and beans are commonly used, occasionally with fresh ginseng root, for a subtle aroma. *Dolsot-bap* is also good when mixed with sesame soy sauce. The combination of chewy rice and roasted sesame oil is heavenly. Seafood or mushroom may be added to make *songi-dolsot-bap* (stone pot rice with pine mushroom) in the autumn, and *gul-bap* (stone pot rice with oysters), *honghap-bap* (stone pot rice with mussels), or *mu-bap* (stone pot rice with white radish) are commonly prepared in the winter. Chopped garden or wild chives may be added to the sesame soy sauce for enhanced flavor. Lastly, the delicious crusty rice layer at the bottom of the stone pot is not to be missed even if it takes some serious spoon work to scrape it off.

An International Healthy Dish
Bibimbap
[*Bibimbap*]

Bibimbap, cooked rice mixed with vegetables, sautéed beef, and *twigak* (dried seaweed or vegetables fried in oil), is one of the definitive Korean dishes in the eyes of both Koreans and international enthusiasts. Once called *goldongban* by the public and *bibim* in the royal palace, *bibimbap* has been one of the most popular in-flight meals around the world since it was first introduced by airlines in the early 1990s.

A Product of Ancestral Rites and Communal Labor

There are three common beliefs about the origin of *bibimbap*. First, it is said to be derived from traditional Korean ancestral rites. Koreans prepare cooked rice, meat, fish, and vegetables for a table offered to the ancestors. The ritual they perform after holding an ancestral rite is called *eumbok*, the partaking of sacrificial food and drink, and *bibimbap* is believed to have stemmed from the practice of mixing *bap* with other dishes for *eumbok*. Some say that *bibimbap* originated from the ancient custom of mixing leftover cooked rice with all the remaining side dishes and eating it as a midnight snack on Lunar New Year's Eve.

Lastly, *bibimbap* could have been inspired by the simple meals farmers consumed in the fields. Koreans have a custom of communally pooling labor when planting rice or harvesting crops. In order to save time and work, everyone would bring some food which would be mixed and shared out on the fields. Every local variation of *bibimbap* has its own unique characteristics depending on the region where it comes from. *Bibimbap* from Jeonju and Jinju is particularly famous.

A Botanical Garden inside the Bowl

Jeonju is very famous for its *kongnamul-bibimbap* (bean sprouts *bibimbap*), an elaborate dish requiring approximately 30 different ingredients. The rice itself is boiled in a stock made with beef brisket, and the dish is topped with a mung bean starch jelly tinted with yellow gardenia juice. *Jeonju-bibimbap* traditionally has *yuk-hoe* (beef tartare) as one of the mixing ingredients, but those unaccustomed to eating uncooked beef can have it with regular sautéed beef. Jinju is famous for its *kkot-bap* (flower *bibimbap*), which conjures up images of a beautiful botanical garden. This version of *bibimbap* is served with a broth made with chopped littleneck clams sautéed in sesame oil.

Heotjesat-bap, an Indelible Taste

Heotjesat-bap (faux-sacrificial *bibimbap*) is a famous local dish in the Gyeongsang Provinces. It is basically a sacrificial *bibimbap* without the actual memorial service. The name comes from tales of *yangbans* (gentry class) faking ancestral rites just to eat this dish. Others say that commoners, who were not allowed to hold memorial services of this style, cooked sacrificial foods just to eat them. The *bap* in *heotjesat-bap* is mixed with soy sauce instead of *gochujang* (red chili paste) and served with a beef and radish broth, *sanjeok* (seasoned beef brochette), *bugeo-jjim* (simmered dried pollack), *dubu-buchim* (pan-fried tofu), *dombaegi-sanjeok* (shark meat brochette), and *namul* (vegetable side dishes).

Sanchae-bibimbap and *Dolsot-bibimbap*

Sanchae-bibimbap (mountain vegetable *bibimbap*) was created when Buddhist monks mixed rice with wild-grown mountain herbs and vegetables. The dish is light and fragrant due to the ingredients which are wild-grown in the mountains.

Dolsot-bibimbap (stone pot rice with vegetables and beef) is characterized by the *nurungji* that sears at the bottom of the pot. It is especially popular because people can listen to the sizzling sound of the residual heat of the pot continuing to cook the rice. The best part of eating this dish is scraping the *nurungji*—the bottom crusty layer of rice—off the stone pot. *Dolsot-bibimbap* is popular among foreigners who sometimes compare the crusty layer to the Socarrat of Spanish paella.

Bibimbap and Hollywood Celebrities

Bibimbap has won the hearts of many Hollywood celebrities. Gywneth Paltrow referred to *bibimbap* as a personal secret on a TV show featuring Hollywood celebrites' weight-loss tips. It caused quite a stir when Paltrow uploaded instructions for making *bibimbap* on her website. Other self-proclaimed *bibimbap* fans include the late Michael Jackson, Paris Hilton, and Nicholas Cage.

Bibimbap as Comfort Food

Nothing is more comforting to Koreans than rice mixed with fiery *gochujang* (red chili paste) and all the leftover dishes rummaged from the refrigerator. Koreans say that the moment a spoonful of *bibimbap* enters your mouth, the bitterness and resentment in your heart starts to melt away. *Bibimbap* is the ultimate comfort food for Koreans, which magically provides relief for heartaches, pent up frustrations, and even stress and anxiety.

Bibimbap Ad in Times Square

In the autumn of 2010, a *bibimbap* advertisement appeared on the electronic billboard in New York's Times Square. The colorful ad was eye-catching and featured a variety of Korean cultural items, such as *nanta*, taekwondo, Samulnori (percussion quartet), Ganggangsuwolle (circle dance), masked dance, and the Bukcheong lion dance.

A rite held for greatly-honored ancestors at an esteemed family's residence called Gyeongdangjong-taek. It is a long-standing tradition for Koreans to eat *bibimbap* during the rite called *eumbok* (partaking of sacrificial food and drink) following a memorial service.

A Full Meal in a Single Roll
Gimbap
[Korean Dried Seaweed Rice Rolls]

Gimbap is made by spreading white rice on a sheet of *gim* (dried laver), layering it with spinach, pickled radish, carrots, egg, and beef, and rolling it up. It is similar to the Japanese *maki* roll but differs in that the rice is seasoned with sesame oil and salt rather than with vinegar, sugar, and salt.

Different Fillings, Different Names

It was in the 1960s and 70s that *gimbap* as we know it—rolled up into a cylindrical form— became popular. The rice-roll was the default picnic lunch for annual spring and autumn school outings. Many Koreans fondly remember eating the end pieces of the rolls while their mother prepared *gimbap* on the morning of school picnics. In the mid-1990s, *gimbap* became an everyday food with the launch of the successful *gimbap* franchise, "Jongno Gimbap." They take *gimbap on* a thick roll with generous portions of rice and novel fillings such as kimchi, sliced processed cheese, perilla leaves, and anything else one fancied. Thus, *gimbap* became ubiquitous, and multiplied into many variations: *cheese-gimbap, tuna-gimbap, kimchi-gimbap,* etc.

Fat Granny's *Chungmu-gimbap*

A unique variation of *gimbap* is the *kkoma-gimbap*, finger-size rolls of rice wrapped in dried laver sheets without any filling and eaten with spicy squid salad and radish kimchi. Its origins date back decades to days when ferries were preferred as a form of transportation over the relatively underdeveloped roads. Passengers used to bring their own *gimbap* to tide them over the long ferry ride. However, the regular *gimbap* with fillings spoiled easily. One elderly woman saw this and started to sell plain rice rolls served with a separate side dish. It was an instant hit. As roads improved and fewer ferries operated, the woman settled down and opened her own place named "Chungmu Gimbap" in Chungmu City. Although Chungmu later merged into Tongyeong as a result of administrative reorganization, the place is still called "Chungmu Gimbap" and has become a famous tourist stop.

A Slice of the Ocean on the Dinner Table: Dried Laver
Called nature's greatest gift, laver is a remarkably nutritious food packed with protein and vitamins. It has been cultivated for ages and is considered at its best when it shows fewer impurities, a darker color and a fuller sheen.

Fortune and Health Wrapped in One
Ssambap
[Leaf Wraps and Rice]

Ssambap is cooked rice and condiments wrapped in fresh greens or seaweed leaves. Koreans have always been extremely skilled at bundling and wrapping things in cloth. It's no wonder Koreans enjoy wrapping food at the table. Wild vegetables, herbs, seafood… Nothing is "unwrappable" as long as it can be placed on a leaf and held in the palm.

Anything Goes

Leafy greens for *ssam* (wraps) often appear on Korean tables: grilled beef is invariably served with *ssam* greens, as well as sliced raw fish (*saengseon-hoe*), which is wrapped with bits of chili pepper or garlic. Pork belly barbecue restaurants always serve *ssam* greens on the side. When the price of greens spikes in the dead heat of summer, sales at pork belly restaurants plummet. No one will go when these restaurants skimp on the greens, because piling up layers of fresh leaves and wrapping it up is half the fun.

Crunchy or Soft

The most common *ssam* wrappers are leafy vegetables, including lettuce, perilla leaves, crown daisy, napa cabbage, and kale. More than ten kinds of lettuce can be used as wraps. Cabbage and curled mallow, which are too tough to eat raw, can be blanched or steamed.

Seaweed such as kelp (*dasima*) and sea mustard (*miyeok*) are also popular ingredients for *ssam*. Boiled meat can be wrapped with kimchi, which is called *bossam*. As *ssambap* employs a variety of seasonal raw vegetables, it conserves all the precious nutrients that help prevent lifestyle diseases such as calcium, iron, and vitamins A and C, which might otherwise be lost in the process of cooking. Since kelp, soybean paste and cooked brown rice are all alkaline foods rich in minerals, eating them helps to neutralize acids and aids digestion.

The Extravagant Version: Royal *Ssambap*

It's allowed to disregard table manners when eating *ssambap*. Even the King would eat this dish with his bare hands. The Royal *ssambap* was served with a wide variety of fillings, ranging from *jang-ttokttogi* (stir-fried julienned beef) and *byeongeo-gamjeong* (pomfret braised with hot pepper paste) to *borisaeu-bokkeum* (small shrimp stir-fry), accompanied with a special sauce of *gochujang*, sautéed ground meat, sesame oil and pine nuts.

Lettuce-*ssambap* for a Good Night's Sleep

Bitter-tasting lettuce usually leaves one feeling drowsy. This is due to a slightly sour substance called lactucarium which is helpful in treating insomnia, jaundice, and anemia. Lettuce also helps reduce bloating, urinary difficulties, achy joints, and turbid blood.

Easy and Delicious
Kimchi-bokkeum-bap

[Kimchi Fried Rice]

Koreans have long savored the combination of *bap* (cooked rice) and kimchi at the table, but it was only after the 1930s that kimchi fried rice emerged on the culinary scene. This was because modern frying pans made it possible to fry finely chopped kimchi and rice in oil.

Bap, Kimchi, Oil and the Frying Pan

Korean-style fried rice was born after Chinese fried rice and Japanese *omurice* became popular in Korea. Inspired by these foreign dishes, Koreans created *kimchi-bokkeum-bap* by making use of their national dish. A simple plate of *kimchi-bokkeum-bap* on its own, cooked with aged, sour kimchi, balances the greasiness of the oil and results in a delicious one-dish meal. This is part of the truism that *bap* and kimchi alone can serve as a meal for Koreans. *Kimchi-bokkeum-bap* is the perfect answer when nothing else is in the fridge, when you're feeling lazy, when nothing seems appetizing, or when there's leftover rice lying around.

If a meal consists of just rice and kimchi, it might be too bare. But *kimchi-bokkeum-bap* transforms two basic items into a complete stand-alone dish with great flavor and visual appeal. This is why *kimchi-bokkeum-bap* enjoys an enduring popularity in Korea.

Kimchi-bokkeum-bap in Full Extravaganza

In early 1990s, *cheolpan-bokkeum-bap* stands were all the rage. The customer selected a few ingredients, and the chef fried them with rice on a flat iron plate, drizzled some sauce on top, and served it on a plate. Kimchi was the ingredient of choice for a majority of customers. So kimchi became the default ingredient, and customers simply picked out the additional ingredients from a selection of meats, vegetables, and seafood.

The Master Key to *Hansik* Pantries: Kimchi
Kimchi appears as a side dish in nearly all *hansik* settings and serves as a culinary silver bullet, freely crossing the border between main courses and side dishes. When used as an ingredient, it can be converted into a variety of new dishes, harmonizing together with *bap, guk, jjigae, tang, jeon, jjim, jorim, bokkeum,* and *jeongol.*

Bulgogi for the Single Diner
Bulgogi-deopbap
[*Bulgogi* with Rice]

Topping steamed rice with *bulgogi* gives you *bulgogi-deopbap*. Similar to the Japanese *don-buri*, *bulgogi-deopbap* is the solution for single diners who don't want the fuss of table-top grilling. It is a convenient dish and very popular among busy urbanites.

An Accessible and Convenient Version of *Bulgogi*

In the old days, meat was so precious that it was only served at banquets or on special occasions. This idea still remains in modern day Korea where the minimum order of *bulgogi* or pork belly is for two, unless it is an extra order. *Bulgogi-deopbap* broke this pre-conceived notion and made *bulgogi* a more accessible dish served in neighborhood restaurants or food stands, as well as a convenient dish for single and/or busy diners.

Reinvented: *Bassak-bulgogi-deopbap*

Bulgogi-deopbap has a juicy sauce that can be mixed with rice. But mixing at the table can become messy. *Bassak-bulgogi-deopbap* solves this problem by draining the juice from the cooked *bulgogi*, stir-frying the rice in it, and serving the two together. This dry *bulgogi* is also good for picnic lunchboxes or for making *bulgogi* sandwiches. Skewered *bassak-bulgogi* is also great for dinner parties.

Bulgogi-deopbap **Recipe**

Bulgogi-deopbap is surprisingly easy to prepare. All you needed is sliced beef, onions, and rice. First, prepare the marinade with 5T soy sauce, 1T sugar, 1T malt syrup (*mulyeot*) or honey, 1/2t crushed roasted sesame seeds, and 1t sesame oil. Mix the marinade with 400g beef and 1/2 onion, both thinly sliced, and let marinate for 30 min. Cook the meat adding 1C water, and pour over a bed of cooked rice.

A Sweet and Spicy Low-fat Dish
Ojingeo-deopbap
[Spicy Stir-fried Squid with Rice]

At restaurants, *jeyuk-deopbap* (spicy stir-fried pork with rice) is the favored one-dish rice meal for hungry men. But most women who want to watch their figures will opt for *ojingeo-deopbap*. This is because *ojingeo-deopbap* is filling yet surprisingly low in calories.

Cabbage and Squid, a Perfect Combination

Compared to red meat, squid is richer in proteins but lower in calories. *Ojingeo-deopbap*, in addition, is pH-balanced, because it combines squid, an acidic food, with alkaline vegetables such as cabbage, onions, and carrots. Cabbage is an additional boon, because it is also low-cal and rich in dietary fiber. With the addition of hot pepper powder and red pepper paste the effect is doubled, because the abundant capsaicin in red pepper helps break down fat. *Ojingeo-deopbap* has every reason to be loved by people trying to stay in shape.

Osam-bulgogi

For those who are torn between healthy squid and satisfying pork, there is a perfect solution called *osam-bulgogi*. It is a dish combining squid and pork belly slices which is stir-fried in a spicy sauce. Koreans commonly face the *Jajangmyeon-Jjamppong Dilemma* where one must choose between black bean noodles (*jajangmyeon*) or spicy soup noodles (*jjamppong*) at a Chinese restaurant. The same dilemma arises with squid and pork, and *osam-bulgogi* solves this problem. It is also good served over steamed rice.

Red Pepper Tea for a Healthy Diet
Making a dish with generous addition of red pepper lowers the total calories by 10 to 20 percent. Thus, red pepper tea is also an effective diet tea. After steeping barley, green or black tea in the normal fashion, add a couple of dried red peppers and boil for approximately three more minutes. It can be stored cool in the refrigerator and drunk like water. It stays fresh for several days.

A Soothing Soup for the Morning After
Kongnamul-gukbap
[Bean Sprout and Rice Soup]

Kongnamul-guk is the first soup the novice cook learns to make. It is also the easiest dish for singles to make. Water, soybean sprouts, salt, and scallion are all that is needed. This soup is simple to cook but tricky to get it to taste exactly right. This clean, mild and refreshing soup is the best breakfast on a morning following a wild night on the town.

Mild and Refreshing Soup

Mung bean sprouts are widely used in Japan and many Southeast Asian countries, but soybean sprouts are only found in Korea. It is well-known that vitamin C, which soy bean lacks, is abundant in the sprouts. One plate of soybean sprouts contains half the recommended daily intake of vitamin C. Soybean sprouts are also rich in asparaginic acid, a type of amino acid, which helps break down alcohol.

Jeonju is famous for its *kongnamul-guk*, because, the city's water is exceptionally clean and fresh. To prepare Jeonju-style *kongnamul-gukbap*, cook rice using less water than normal, spoon rice into an earthen bowl and pour in the soup. Thick-stemmed soybean sprouts should be used. Immediately before eating, season it with the clear juice from salted shrimp (*saeujeot*).

Kongnamul-guk as a Cold Remedy

Some Koreans add an egg to *kongnamul-gukbap*, and the soup is soon muddied with the broken yolk. In Jeonju, only the egg white or a pre-cooked poached egg (*suran*)* is added. Drinkers often claim that the best way to enjoy *kongnamul-gukbap* is eating it with *moju*, a crude liquor made by thoroughly boiling *makgeolli* (Korean rice wine) with ginger, cinnamon, and jujubes. Alternating between the hot soup and sips of *moju* is supposed to induce sweat and effectively cure any hangover. This is, however, a misperception. Drinking *moju* in fact only raises the alcohol level in the body.

Other than curing hangovers, *kongnamul-guk* is also good for colds. The plentiful vitamin C in the soup does wonders for a heavy cold or 24-hour flu. Since the old days, Koreans have eased their cold symptoms by slurping hot *kongnamul-guk* with a generous sprinkling of red chili powder.

* *Suran* is an egg dropped into boiling water and soft-boiled without breaking the yolk.

Bean sprouts (*kongnamul*) contain a substance that enhances the supply of oxygen to the brain, and the improved nourishment then boosts brain function.

Rich and Nutty Taste

Jat-juk

[Pine Nut Porridge]

Everyone loves *jat-juk* because of its velvety texture and fragrant smell. This porridge was once reserved as a restorative food for the sick or elderly, or as breakfast for important guests, not only because of its aromatic and nutty flavor, but also because pine nuts were a rare and expensive ingredient.

Velvety Smooth with Pine Nut Fragrance

In the royal palace, the King and the Queen were served with a bowl of different *juks* in bed as a pre-breakfast (*jari-joban*) on days they did not receive herbal tonics. *Jat-juk* was considered to be the best of all porridges. Although this dish often appears in documents from the Joseon Dynasty, its origin has never been traced. Two or three parts pine nuts to one part rice is used to make *jat-juk*. In order to enhance the flavor of the pine nuts, the pine nuts and rice should be finely ground beforehand. When boiling, a wooden spoon or paddle must be used for stirring, because otherwise the porridge can quickly turn watery. This will also happen if salt is added before serving.

Pine nuts are already rich in protein and healthy fats, but some people add roasted sesame seeds to further enhance the flavor. Buddhist monks who are on vegetarian fasts or go days without sleep often eat *jat-juk*, served with *dongchimi* (radish water kimchi), to increase energy and restore lost appetite. When making *jat-juk*, the rice and pine nuts should be separately puréed with water. The clear liquids from the rice purée and pine nut purée are poured off, combined, and boiled together. Then the rice sediment is added followed by the pine nut sediment. The mixture is cooked until it reaches a thick consistency.

Heugimja-juk, **the Elixer of Youth**
Along with *jat-juk*, *heugimja-juk* (black sesame porridge) is another popular breakfast dish. It was also served as a pre-breakfast to the King. Black sesame is rich in vitamin E and lecithin, which are antioxidants and help keep the skin youthful. Perhaps this was why *heugimja-juk* was an important diet of the *hwarang* (elite youth corps) warriors of the Silla Kingdom, as they placed great importance on grooming.

A Sweet Dish Served as Appetizer or Dessert
Hobak-juk
[Pumpkin Porridge]

Although summer squash and winter squash can both be used, *hobak-juk* is typically made with winter squash, or pumpkin. The bright orange color and soft sweetness of the pumpkin make *hobak-juk* a visual and gastronomic delight, and a popular dish that can be served either as a first course or dessert.

The Pumkin Rolls in, Vine and All!

Squash was introduced to Korea after the Japanese invasion of 1592. Its original name was *seungso*, which means "vegetable of the monks." This was because Buddhist monks often cultivated squash on the temple grounds. There were no dedicated squash fields in old times, since the plants grew so well along the walls or any corner of the back yard. Each part of the squash plant is edible, including the flesh, leaf, and sprout. *Hobak-namul* (sautéed zucchini), *hobak-kimchi* (winter squash *kimchi*), *hobak-jeon* (pan-fried zucchini), and *hobak-jjim* (steamed winter squash) are all dishes made from squash. Dishes made from winter squash, or pumpkins, include *hobak-tteok* (pumpkin rice cake), *hobak-beombeok* (pumpkin and mixed grain porridge), and *hobak-juk* (pumpkin porridge) which mostly consumed as snacks. The value of squash, or pumpkin, led to the Korean expression "A whole pumpkin rolled into the house, vine and all!" which means to be blessed with a great prize or catch. *Hobak-juk* has long been a favorite wintertime source of vitamins. There is even a saying, "Eat pumpkin on the winter solstice to prevent having a stroke."

Hobak-juk contains a lot of carotene, which converts to vitamin A when absorbed by the body. Pumpkins are also low in calories, thus good for weight-control. The many vitamins and minerals in pumpkin have anti-aging properties, while the dietary fiber helps to prevent constipation and keeps the skin clear and smooth. Contrary to the Korean expression that compares unattractive women to "pumpkins," pumpkins are actually wonderful for promoting youth and beauty.

Hobak-juk Recipe
Rinse sweet pumpkin well, place in a pot, pour in just enough water to cover it, and boil until soft. Remove from heat and scrape out the flesh. Mix with sweet rice powder and simmer for a while. Add soaked beans and continue to cook. This smooth and sweet-tasting porridge is beneficial for the elderly or recovering patients. Another interesting variation is made by thickening the porridge by adding rice balls (*sae-al*) which are made by mixing sweet rice powder with hot water and shaping them into small balls.

A Jewel from the Ocean
Jeonbok-juk
[Abalone Rice Porridge]

The Chinese emperor Qin Shi Huang (206-210BC), who desired eternal life, is known to have consumed abalone as an elixir. Abalone was precious in old Korea and was always one of the tribute goods offered to the King. Nowadays, farmed abalones are more readily available. And *jeonbok-juk* is still the first thing people will make when a family member falls sick.

A Source of Many Nutrients

Abalones feed on mineral-rich seaweeds such as sea mustard and kelp. Thus, the abalone is believed to embody "the vitality of the ocean." Abalone is a popular health food, rich in proteins and vitamins as well as minerals such as calcium and phosphorus. The milky soup of *jeonbok-juk* combined with the firm texture of bits of abalone flesh tastes wonderful, and has a savory flavor that envelops the palate.

Abalone Entrails, a Delicacy of the Ocean

Jeong Yak-jeon, a Joseon Dynasty scholar, introduced abalones in 1814 in his book *Jasaneo-bo**: "The succulent flesh of the abalone tastes good both raw and grilled, but the best way to enjoy it is to slice and dry it. Abalone entrails can be boiled and salted."

Jeonbok-hoe (sliced fresh abalone) or grilled abalones have a chewy texture that tantalizes the mouth. When grilled or parboiled in shell, the flesh shrinks slightly and becomes tender. The abalone entrails are loved by gourmets who appreciate the intense flavor. Abalone entrails, called *Ga-ut* or *Ge-u* in Korean, have a green tint when the abalone is male and a yellow tint in the case of females.

When preparing *jeonbok-juk*, the addition of entrails is the only way to obtain the deep ocean flavor. Another way to enjoy the entrails is to mix it with vegetables and season it with vinegared *gochujang*. The result is a unique, fishy flavored dish. Salted abalone entrails were considered a rare delicacy reserved for important guests. Unshelled abalones can be put in a kettle of *soju* to produce a green-tinted abalone liquor which is known to stimulate the appetites. Nevertheless, the first and foremost abalone dish in Korea is *jeonbok-juk*. It is so tasty that some say the dish was created to allow as many people as possible to savor the taste of precious abalones.

* *Jasaneobo* (Fishes of Heuksan Island) is the oldest surviving record of marine life in Korea, written in 1814 by the Joseon scholar Jeong Yak-jeon, who personally compiled the name, appearance, behavior, usage, etc. of 155 different species of marine life from the coastal waters surrounding Heuksan Island, South Jeolla Province.

Yellowish Wild Abalones and Greenish Farmed Abalones
Wando Island and Jeju Island are both famous for abalones. Wild abalone refers to those hand-harvested by traditional female divers. They are yellowish in color, while farmed ones tend more greenish. The flesh of wild abalones, about the size of an adult's palm, is very elastic and firm, difficult to chew unless you have strong teeth. Nevertheless, this unique texture has captivated the palates of gourmets.

MYEON & GUKSU

[Noodles and Dumplings]

In Korea, we have a saying "noodles instead of rice." This shows how noodles, or *guksu*, were an integral part of our diet. *Guksu* is enjoyed on auspicious occasions such as birthdays, the 60th birthday celebration, and weddings, and denotes a message of congratulations. It is a light and simple food that is easy to prepare and consume.

Icy Cold and Exhilarating
Mul-naengmyeon
[Cold Buckwheat Noodles]

Koreans usually cite *bulgogi* as their favorite wintertime dish and *naengmyeon* for the summertime. There are two main types of *mul-naengmyeon*: Pyeongyang-style and Hamheung-style. *Pyeongyang naengmyeon* is characterized by softer noodles due to a larger content of buckwheat, and a clear and mild-flavored broth. *Hamheung naengmyeon* contains a higher percentage of potato or sweet potato starch, resulting in a more firm and stringy texture. The taste is enhanced by adding generous dollops of vinegar and mustard to the broth.

Cold Noodles, Warm Toes

Nowadays, *naengmyeon* is considered a summer food, but in the old days, the *naengmyeon* experience was a combination of an *ondol* (underfloor heating system), freezing winter temperature, and icy-cold *naengmyeon*. The broth was made with *dongchimi* (radish water *kimchi*) brine scooped out of the earthenware crock which was half-buried in the ground for winter storage. No one knows exactly when Koreans started to eat *naengmyeon*. However, based on the fact that buckwheat was introduced by the Mongol Empire during the Goryeo Dynasty, one can assume that people living in the mountainous North Korean region first began eating it around that time.

A Taste of Home

For the older generation North Korean, *naengmyeon* is a nostalgic reminder of the home left behind. *Naengmyeon* was initially a specialty of the northern regions, but became popular across the country when North Korean fled to the South during the Korean War. Having few means to support themselves, many displaced North Korean began to make and sell *naengmyeon*. It is common to see a number of elderly North Korean gathered in *naengmyeon* restaurants. They are regular customers who come to savor the taste of "home" to which they will probably never return. That is why *naengmyeon* restaurants are bustling with the loud sound of people talking in thick northern accents, something that is hard to hear elsewhere.

North Korea, the origin of *naengmyeon*, still maintains its reputation. In North Korea, they say, "You can't claim to have been in Pyeongyang unless you've tasted *naengmyeon* at Okryugwan." The Okryugwan is a landmark restaurant famous for its *naengmyeon*, and is always on the list of places to visit for dignitaries and even South Korean visitors. It is said that the late Kim Il-sung, the former "Great Leader" of North Korea, instructed that the distinctive taste of *okryugwan naengmyeon* be preserved forever.

Mild Pyeongyang vs. Sweet and Spicy Hamheung

The broth used in *pyeongyang naengmyeon* is made by simmering beef, pheasant, or chicken and combining it with the brine of well-fermented *baechu-kimchi* (cabbage kimchi) or *dongchimi*. The noodles are served with garnishes such as *pyeonyuk* (pressed boiled meat), julienned cucumbers and pears, and hard-boiled eggs. To fully enjoy the subtle-flavored broth, only a small amount of vinegar and mustard should be added. Meanwhile, *hamheung naengmyeon* is served with a spicy sauce that goes well with the stringy noodles. Adding ample vinegar and mustard can even enhance the taste further. It's always a good idea to eat the boiled egg first, in order to soften the blow of the fiery sauce.

Spicy with Lasting Flavor
Bibim-naengmyeon
[Spicy Buckwheat Noodles]

Among the many variations on *bibim-naengmyeon, hamheung naengmyeon* topped with *hoe* (sliced fresh fish) is the most famous. North Korean usually like their food mild, but this *naengmyeon* is an exception. *Hoe-naengmyeon* (cold buckwheat noodles with raw fish) tastes best with plenty of vinegar and mustard. In integral part of the meal is to intermittently sip the steaming hot beef broth (*yuksu*) to soothe the burning mouth.

Stringy Noodles and Hot Sauce

The coastal Hamheung area has long provided bountiful fishing for brown sole (*gajami*). People around the region enjoy sliced raw sole with spicy *gochujang* sauce. When the so-called *hoe-muchim* (seasoned sliced fresh fish) is placed on *naengmyeon*, it creates the popular *hoe-naengmyeon*. Stringy noodles made with potato starch harmonize perfectly with the spicy seasoned fish. After the Korean War, *hoe-naengmyeon* was introduced to South Korea by North Korean refugees. As the available ingredients differed from those of Hamgyeong Province, the noodles were made with sweet potato starch from Jeju Island instead of potato starch, and sole, the original ingredient for garnishing, was replaced with skate or stingray.

War refugees who had to flee south to Busan from the North returned to Seoul after the war and settled in Ojang-dong near Jangchung-dong where the government building for North Koreans was located. Since then, *hamheung naengmyeon* restaurants opened one after another, and the area is now dubbed the "*Hamheung Naengmyeon Alley*."

Myeonsu and *Yuksu*

One of the key differences between *pyeongyang naengmyeon* and *hamheung naengmyeon* is whether they serve noodle broth or meat broth. After taking an order, authentic *pyeongyang naengmyeon* houses serve *myeonsu* (water in which noodles were boiled) in a teacup. The hot water brimming with the toasty aroma of buckwheat is one of the best parts of going to a *naengmyeon* restaurant. Meanwhile, *hamheung naengmyeon* restaurants serve hot *yuksu* (meat broth) rather than *myeonsu*. Many elderly people will order a bottle of *soju* (distilled spirit) with *suyuk* (boiled beef slices) and sip on the hot broth as an accompaniment to their drinks.

Bibim-naengmyeon is divided into two classes: *naengmyeon* with pressed boiled meat (*pyeonyuk*) and sliced fresh fish (hoe). Falling between the two, there is an interesting dish known as *saekkimi-naengmyeon*. The word *saekkimi* is from North Korean dialect and means "mixing several things together." It is topped with beef and slices of fresh fish and allows people to taste both in a single bowl of *naengmyeon*. *Originally, Hoe-naengmyeon* was garnished with fresh sole, but today stingray is commonly used.

A Dish for Special Days
Janchi-guksu
[Banquet Noodles]

Janchi-guksu is noodles in a hot clear *jang-guk*, or beef broth. Although *janchi-guksu* is now commonly available, it was originally served only on special occasions due to the scarcity of wheat flour. Noodles were also served at auspicious events because the long strands symbolized longevity.

For Wedding Days

Janchi-guksu has long been a classic food for serving guests on special occasions. In particular, noodles were invariably served at weddings to wish the newlyweds lasting love. Koreans will often say "I'm going to eat *guksu*" instead of saying they are going to a wedding. And if one asks "When will you treat me to a bowl of *guksu*?", it actually means "When are you planning to get married?"

There was a time when people considered it more prestigious to serve wedding guests *galbitang* (short rib soup) rather than *janchi-guksu*. This was because people started to prefer expensive beef from the 1980s. These days, however, people have gone back to *janchi-guksu* out of respect for the original meaning of celebration and longevity. At home, *janchi-guksu* is served with seasoned soy sauce and sautéed zucchini. *Janchi-guksu* for banquet, however, is more elaborate with colorful garnishes such as sautéed meat, pan-fried egg garnishes, sautéed stone ear mushrooms *(seogi)*, and Korean parsley *(minari)*.

Dried Anchovy Stock Replaces Meat Broth

As its alternate name "*jangguk-guksu* or *jangguksu*" demonstrates, *janchi-guksu* was originally made with *jangguk*, or a meat broth. Recently, however, *myeolchi-guksu* (noodles in dried anchovy stock) has been enjoying greater popularity. Here *jangguk* refers to a broth resulting from stir-frying finely-chopped beef and boiling it in water. *Janchi-guksu* is easy to consume and the clear broth is pleasing to the palate. Together with *gukbap* (rice in soup), noodles served in *jangguk* used to be the most popular food eaten in the outdoor markets that opened every five days. Hundreds of bowls of noodles could easily be prepared as long as you had plenty of broth in the pot, pre-cooked and drained noodles, and a few garnishes at hand. The broth is poured into the bowl and drained three times to heat the pre-boiled noodles. This action is called *toryeom*.

How to Cook Perfect Noodles
Pour plenty of water into a large pot or cauldron, add the noodles, and keep stirring until it boils. Once it boils, add a bowl of cold water to cool it down. After boiling a little longer, strain and rinse the noodles in cold water. The more you rinse in cold water, the smoother and the more elastic the noodles become as the starch is washed away. A well-prepared and delicately arranged garnish can make *janchi-guksu* suitable for even the finest table or special guests.

A Spicy Meal that Wakes up the Senses
Bibim-guksu
[Spicy Noodles]

Bibim-guksu was originally made with soy sauce. It was a dish of the royal cuisine, and thus made with lavish ingredients. The *dongguksesigi* (Korean Almanac),* complied in 1849, introduces the original of modern *bibim-guksu* and describes it as "buckwheat noodles mixed with a variety of vegetables, pear, chestnut, beef, pork, sesame oil and soy sauce, and called by the name of *goldongmyeon*."

Spicy *Bibim-guksu* Appears Only after the War

The word *goldong* contains a meaning of mixing different things together. *Sieuijeonseo,** a cookbook first compiled in 1919, describes how to cook *goldongmyeon*: "Marinate minced beef and stir-fry. Parboil mung bean sprouts and Korean parsley and then mix with jelly (*muk*) and seasoning sauce. Mix everything with cooked noodles and place in a bowl. Garnish with stir-fried beef, and sprinkle with red pepper and crushed roasted sesame seeds. Set dish on the table with clear beef broth."

Both *Dongguksesigi* and *Sieuijeonseo* indicate that *bibim-guksu* made with beef, vegetables, and seasonings, was a special treat. Even so, *goldongmyeon* was made of buckwheat, which means that wheat flour was not easily available even in the royal palace. It was only when wheat flour became widely available after the Korean War that we began to eat wheat flour noodles mixed with *gochujang* and *kimchi*, as a dish today known as *bibim-guksu*.

* *Dongguksesigi* is a record of seasonal customs by Hong Seok-mo, a scholar from the late Joseon Period. The book details the annual events and customs of Joseon Society.

* *Sieuijeonseo* is a cookbook from the late 19th century. Its author is unknown. The book categorized and organized the traditional Korean food of the late Joseon period and is known as the literature where *bibimbap* appears.

Particularly Good for the Sweltering Days of Summer
Bibim-guksu is popular mainly in the summertime. It's generous portion of cucumbers cools down an overheated body and quenches thirst, helping relieve swelling by serving as a diuretic.

A Heap of Noodles on a Large Platter
Jaengban-guksu
[Jumbo Sized Buckwheat Noodles]

Jaengban-guksu has been popular since the 1990's when *mak-guksu* (mixed buckwheat noodles) restaurants first began to offer 2-3 portion of *mak-guksu* on large platters, with mounds of delectable garnishes. The noodles, mixed with spicy sauce, fall somewhere between *bibim-guksu* and *bibim-naengmyeon*.

Mixing and Sharing—the Korean Way

Jaengban-guksu literally means "platter noodle." One may wonder why noodles are served on a platter instead of individual bowls. But that's the key point. *Jaengban-guksu* is basically *bibim-guksu* on a platter. Mixed with several kinds of vegetables, *jaengban-guksu* epitomizes the Korean style of dining: mixing and sharing. The Korean practice of eating from the same dish signifies trust and intimacy. Another merit of *jaengban-guksu* is that individuals can eat as much or little as they want.

The *Jaengban-guksu* Diet

Jaengban-guksu is best described as a dish made of "half noodles, half vegetables." The vegetables include lettuce, crown daisy, cucumber, and carrot. Boiled beef and eggs are also tossed in, but the main ingredient is definitely vegetables. It is a low-fat, low-calorie meal and perfect for weight-watchers. No one can know who ate how much vegetables or noodles. *Jaengban-guksu* is definitely the best way to diet without letting others know.

Memil (buckwheat)
The main ingredient in *jaengban-guksu*, contains ten to twelve percent protein. Most of all, the abundance of essential amino acids such as lysine and tryptophan, which are lacking in most other grains, makes it one of the most nutritious foods.

From Famine Food to Healthy Food
Memil-guksu
[Buckwheat Noodle]

In Korean traditional medicine *memil* is used to make a variety of foods such as *muk*, *naeng-myeon*, *mak-guksu*, *chongtteok*, *jeon*, *sujebi*, and so on. In the past, buckwheat used to be a main ingredient for most of the noodle dishes due to the scarcity of wheat flour. At special occasions like weddings or other celebration events, they usually served grains or food to their guests, and *memil-guksu* was the most frequently served banquet dish. Unlike wheat flour noodle, boiled *memil-guksu* hardly gets soggy so it was an ideal dish for the guests. It was usually served in a hot broth made of meat with garnishes.

Famine Food or Emergency Food

Buckwheat plants were consumed as one of famine foods or emergency foods during the hunger season in spring since the plants grow well even in barren soil or during drought conditions.

The records say that under the reign of King Injo in the Joseon Dynasty, the Korean peninsula was barren after the Japanese invasion of Korea, the Imjin War. People suffered from the years of famine and barely fed themselves with roots of herbs and barks of trees, and the government encouraged them to grow buckwheat as a means of making a living. An old document says that the Joseon people ate buckwheat noodles by pressing the flour batter through the holes on a gourd dipper into boiling water and cooling down the noodle strings. Another record says that *memil-guksu* originated from *memil-sujebi* (soup with roughly torn dough) that mountain field farmers or slash and burn farmers in the Taebaek Mountains ate. Buckwheat was a special grain that appeased people's hunger.

Healthy Food

Buckwheat boasting high quality and taste is harvested in the cool and higher ground, and the products of the Hamgyeong and Gangwon provinces are famous in Korea. It was ground into flour for storage since grain storage techniques were not developed yet in the old days. Buckwheat flour is rich in digestive enzymes and it can be cooked and served for those who are sensitive and have indigestion problems.

In *Bonchogangmok*, the Korean botanical list, it says buckwheat strengthens the stomach, boosts one's energy and helps to eliminate waste matter from the five viscera. *Donguibogam* also describes that buckwheat facilitates digestion so that it even gets rid of a long term dyspepsia. Besides, it can serve as a digestive medicine when one has an upset stomach in the midsummer heat and also as effective anthelmintic because it is the richest source of rutin. Most people have *naengmyeon* after eating *suyuk* (boiled pork), *jokbal* (Korean pork knuckle), or *galbi* because buckwheat helps digestion. Since it gained popularity as a healthy food effective for adult diseases like high blood pressure, buckwheat has been treated as an inexpensive but important grain.

An Excellent Summer Heat Beater
Kong-guksu
[Noodles in Cold Soybean Soup]

Kong-guksu is a seasonal delicacy eaten during the hot summer, and served with noodles in soy milk, which is made by grinding soaked soybeans finely. Tasty and highly nutritious, *kong-guksu* is an energy boosting food in the middle of summer. A big bowl of *kong-guksu*, served with chewy and snow-white wheat flour noodles in soy milk and shredded cucumber on top, which will prevent one from getting an upset stomach while eating in a hurry, is surely an excellent summer heat beater.

The Strong Synergy Between Soybeans and Wheat

Soybeans had originated from Manchuria and are very rich in protein that they are often called "the beef of the fields." Since the old days, Koreans have made various kinds of foods including fermented bean paste, bean curd, bean sprouts, and so on, using soybeans. These days, soybeans are considered one of the best healthy foods. *Donguibogam* describes soybeans as an effective food for treating anger, so it helps people calm down when they are nervous or stressed out. Wheat flour is called *somack* and an ideal food for the summer season because it helps to get rid of a fever and thirst, and have a healthy urination habit. So when wheat flour and soybean are consumed together in one dish, they create a synergy and make a nutritionally excellent food. Since *kong-guksu* is made of soybeans and wheat flour, it has a good food compatibility.

Tastes Much Sweeter than Milk

No written records tell exactly when Koreans started to enjoy *kong-guksu*, but according to *Siuijeonseo*, a cookbook compiled in the late 1800s, "*kong-guk* is made by boiling soaked soybean and pressing it through a fine sieve. It is seasoned with salt and served with wheat flour noodles and garnishes with cold ground sesame on top." It shows the old recipe of *kong-guksu* is similar to that of present one. In order to make delicious *kong-guksu*, the cooking time for soaking and boiling soybeans is critical. If not boiled properly, soybeans are inedible because of the unpleasant raw smell of beans. On the other hand, if boiled too long, they smell like fermented soybean lumps.

The sweet taste of *kong-guk*, which is made by peeling carefully off the long soaked beans, boiling them properly and then grinding them on a millstone, is much better than that of milk. Served with noodles in thick and cool soy milk, *kong-guksu* is an excellent summer heat beater as well as a delicacy providing sufficient water and nutrition. Recently people increase a sweet taste by adding other grains or nuts like sesame, pine, peanut, and walnut to *kong-guksu*, or try to make a new taste with black beans and black sesame. It can make a different kind of health food according to the ingredients added to soy milk.

Made with the Loving Care of a Mother
Kalguksu
[Noodle Soup]

The noodles used for *kalguksu* are made by rolling out wheat flour dough and cutting it with a knife. It is an interesting dish with various styles, taste, and even different degrees of formality. Traditionally, chicken was used for broth in the farmlands, while littleneck clams were used in coastal areas, and dried anchovies in mountainous regions.

Hot *Kalguksu*, Originally a Summer Meal

In the past, wheat was so scarce that people had to wait for the wheat harvest to eat *kalguksu*. Wheat was usually harvested in the middle of the sixth lunar month, thus *kalguksu* was a seasonal delicacy for mid-summer. Potatoes and zucchini are almost always included, since they are also in season at that time of the year. The broth is usually made with ox bone, dried anchovies, or chicken, but can also be made with mushrooms or littleneck clams. In the Jeolla provinces, *pat-kalguksu* (noodle soup with red bean) is very popular.

Geonjin-guksu, a Specialty of the Andong Gentry Households

Geonjin-guksu (drained noodles) was a summertime delicacy formerly made in the Andong region of North Gyeongsang Province. The name comes from the fact that the cooked noodles are rinsed in cold water and then drained. The *yangbans* (gentries) of Andong, who particularly concerned themselves with formalities and saving face, customarily served *geonjin-guksu* to guests. Andong was a relatively secluded area without much commerce with the outside world. The land produced little, and families were generally impoverished. But the *yangban* families could not afford to lose face by neglecting the many houseguests that came and went. And *geonjin-guksu* was created to as a way to be hospitable with what they had. It is made by mixing three parts wheat flour with one part bean flour, rolling it out until it's paper-thin, and meticulously cutting it into thin noodles. The boiled and drained noodles are served in a broth made from sweetfish or beef.

Kalguksu, the President's Favorite Meal
There was a period when *kalguksu* was frequently served at Cheongwadae (the presidential office and residence). President Kim Young-sam, who held office from 1993 to 1998, relished *kalguksu* so much that the chef of Kim's favorite *kalgulsu* restaurant had to teach the the Cheongwadae cooks her recipes. During President Kim's term, guests to official functions at the presidential residence were often dined on a steaming bowl of *kalguksu*.

A Special Dish that Dates Back to Goryeo Dynasty
Mandu
[Dumplings]

Mandu is made by placing a filling of ground meat and vegetables onto a round, thinly rolled wrapper and sealing the edges. They were initially prepared for ancestral rites or banquets and enjoyed as a special dish for the cold of winter. *Mandu* boiled in beef broth is called *mandu-guk* (dumpling soup); *mandu* steamed and served without broth is called *jjin-mandu* (steamed dumplings); and *mandu* served in chilled beef broth is called *pyeonsu* (summer dumplings).

Invented by an Ingenious Military Strategist

Mandu is a Chinese dish attributed to Zhuge Liang.* When Zhuge Liang was returning to his homeland after the conquering the southern regions, he and his troops were prevented from crossing a river by strong currents and high winds. He was advised that the god of the river was expressing his anger, and they would be allowed to safely cross the river if 49 human heads were offered as a military strategist sacrifice. Zhuge Liang refused to sacrifice innocent people and instead made balls of wheat dough stuffed with beef and mutton in the shape of human heads. He offered them to the god of the river, and before too long, the river became calm. The people of southern China came to believe that the offering of Zhuge Liang appeased the river god, and they gave it the name of *mandu*, which means "deceptive head." Another theory claims that *mandu* means "heads in south China." Either way, after that event, the dumplings in the shape of human heads spread to the northern regions and became one of the most representative Chinese dishes. It also spread to Korea and Japan, and now dumplings are enjoyed in all three countries.

Mandu, Much Loved by the Goryeo People

When discussing the origin of Korean dumplings, a famous folk song called "*ssanghwajeom*" (dumpling shop) from the Goryeo Dynasty is frequently mentioned. The song describes how Uyghur people arrived and opened dumpling shops, and how the people of the day greatly enjoyed the dish. However, the lyrics of the song are somewhat suggestive. One verse from the song can be translated as "A woman went to the dumpling shop to buy some dumplings. The Mongolian owner grabbed her hand. If this story gets around, I'll assume that you, the errand boy, spread it. If this gets around, other women will want to go there to sleep with the owner. The place the woman lay down was really cozy and packed."

Some people refer to the song and joke that the Mongol who opened the dumpling shop in Gaeseong (the capital of the Goryeo Dynasty) in 1279 during the rule of King Chungryeol may have been the first foreign direct investor in Korea.

* Zhuge Liang (181–234) was a military strategist and statesman from the state of Shu Han during the Three Kingdoms period in Chinese history. Zhuge Liang helped Liu Bei to totally defeat Cao Cao's forces in an alliance with Sun Quan at the battle known as the "Battle of Red Cliffs."

GUK & TANG

[Soups]

Enjoying a soup or stew together with rice is one of the most fundamental features of Korean dining. There is a unique expression describing the taste of piping hot soup, which is "*siwonhada*". The term literally means "It's cool," but it describes the feeling of hot soup soothing the throat and clearing the chest. *Guk* and *tang* can taste clear, spicy, refreshing, and savory. Along with rice and side dishes, soups are an essential component of a Korean meal.

Soup Made with Healthy Soybean Paste
Doenjang-guk
[Soybean Paste Soup]

Doenjang-guk is a soup made from a special fermented bean paste (*doenjang*) and meat, seafood, or vegetables. It is a marriage of healthy soybean paste with nutritious vegetables rich in fiber and vitamins. Also called *tojang-guk*.

Doenjang from the Birthplace of the Soybean

Soybeans are believed to have originated in the southern part of Manchuria, in the historical territory of Goguryeo (one of the ancient Korean kingdoms). This means that Korea is most likely birthplace of the soybean. The cultivation of soybeans in Korea dates back to at least 4,000 years ago. Koreans also enjoy a long history of eating *doenjang*, made by fermenting soybeans. Our ancestors believed that the tastiest *doenjang* is made on the Malnal (the day of the horse according to the Chinese zodiacal signs) of the first month of the lunar calendar. It might seem that there is some profound source behind this belief, but as a matter of fact, the reason is rather simple: they believed that Daknal (the day of chicken) and Malnal (the day of horse) must be the best days for making *doenjang* because Daknal is pronounced similarly to "*dalda*" (sweet) and Malnal sounds like "*masitda*" (delicious). These days were chosen from among the first twelve days of the Lunar New Year. If they missed the first Malnal, they waited for the next Malnal to come around. There are also other theories as to why *doenjang* was made on the day of the horse. Some say it's because soybeans—the main ingredient in *doenjang*— is a favorite food of horses. Others claim it represents the hope that the color of the *doenjang* appear as rich as horse's blood. *Doenjang* was not just a foodstuff; it was a sacred thing. Therefore, people avoided any impurities starting three days before making it and washed themselves thoroughly on the day of preparation. It is said that women even made *doenjang* with their mouths covered with paper in order to keep the sauce from being tainted with any negative energy coming out of their lips.

The Centenarians' Secret to Longevity
Recently, soybean paste has been a focus of global attention as a healthy condiment rich in functional compounds that are anti-cancerous. In a survey taken among Koreans over 100 years old, 94.9 percent of the respondents said they eat *doenjang-guk* at least once per day.

The Traditional Birthday Treat
Miyeok-guk
[Seaweed Soup]

Miyeok-guk is a symbol of birthdays for Koreans. By custom, it is the first meal mothers eat after giving birth, so it has become a food representing birth. Even those who dislike *miyeok-guk* usually eat it on their birthdays.

The First Meal after Childbirth

It is said that after a baby whale is born, *miyeok* (sea mustard) becomes scarce in the ocean, because the mother whale eat up all the seaweed in order to recover her strength. In Korea, there is a custom of serving mothers *miyeok-guk* and rice as their first meal after childbirth. This soup, which is known as *cheot-gukbap* (the first soup), is clear and seasoned only with soy sauce and sesame oil, as opposed to ordinary *miyeok-guk* which contains beef. When buying dried *miyeok* to make soup for a new mother, one should choose wide and uncut sheets of *miyeok* and not quibble over the price. Due to a popular belief that folding and cutting the long sheets can cause a difficult labor, *miyeok* for post-partum recovery is customarily carried without folding and is bound with a straw rope.

A Popular Dish at the *Jjimjilbang*

Rich in calcium and iodine, *miyeok* helps the womb contract and stimulates the production of new blood cells. Ever since this benefit was first proven scientifically, the Hollywood Presbyterian Medical Center, a well-known Los Angeles hospital, has started to offer *miyeok-guk* as a post-partum meal. At the hospital, the soup has become popular not only among women recovering from delivery, but also with breastfeeding mothers and other patients. *Miyeok-guk* is also believed to promote a more radiant appearance. The soup can be found in nearly every *jjimjilbang* (Korean-style spa/sauna).

A Taboo on Exam Days

When someone says "I ate *miyeok-guk*," it can be translated in two ways. One is "it was my birthday," and the other is "I failed an exam." *Miyeok-guk* can represent failure because the seaweed's slipperiness brings to mind slipping up and failing an exam.

Miyeok-ongsimi

A one-dish meal called *miyeok-ongsimi* can be made as a variation to *miyeok-guk*. It is prepared by adding *saealsim* to *miyeok-guk*. *Saealsim* are small balls made from sweet rice kneaded with hot water. From ancient times, the elderly have enjoyed warm *miyeok-ongsimi* as a way to stimulate the appetite and invigorate the body. *Saealsim* are also often added to *pat-juk* (red bean porridge) or *hobak-juk* (pumpkin porridge).

A Tasty Hangover Cure

Bugeo-guk

[Dried Pollack Soup]

The soup most popular with Korean partygoers also happens to be one of the easiest to prepare for home chefs on a hectic morning. It is *bugeo-guk*. People who have overindulged love it, as the clear stock immediately soothes a stomach upset with alcohol. It is a quick dish and only requires some well-dried pollack.

Take It Out on the Fish

The key to making delicious dried pollack soup is to thoroughly beat a whole dried pollack with a mallet or rolling pin to soften the dried flesh. After this tenderizing process, the fish is descaled and deboned, and torn into pieces, macerated, and boiled. In Korean soap operas, wives are often portrayed cooking *bugeo-guk* early in the morning for a hungover husband. The wife's mixed feelings toward her husband are dramatized as she vents her anger by pounding the fish with all of her might, while endeavoring to ease his hangover with the warm soup.

Air Dried Pollack

In Korea, there is no fish with as many names as the pollack. Freshly-caught pollack is called *saengtae*, frozen pollack is *dongtae*, the salted version is *yeomtae*, and the one that has been frozen and thawed over twenty times during winter is called *hwangtae*. Even dried pollack has multiple names: a fully-grown pollack dried for roughly 60 days is called *bugeo*, a young dried pollack is called *nogari*, while a half-dried fish is referred to as *kodari*.

Among all of these, the one used in making hangover soup is *bugeo*. Nowadays, *hwangtae*, the flesh of which becomes yellowish and swollen due to the multiple temperature changes, is commonly used for the soup as well. Dried pollack can sometimes taste plain because it is less fatty than other fish. However, with a surplus of methionine that supports the liver, it helps to restore livers damaged by excessive drinking.

To make the richest possible *bugeo-guk*, beat a whole pollack with a mallet or rolling pin to soften the dried flesh, pull apart into course strips, and bring to a boil. Make sure to include the head.

Sweating Brings Out the Flavor
Yukgaejang
[Spicy Beef Soup]

Along with ginseng chicken soup and croaker, *yukgaejang* is one of the most popular dishes enjoyed on hot summer days. A bowl of hot and spicy *yukgaejang* on a summer day will bring out the sweat, but it will leave one feeling satisfied and invigorated. *Yukgaejang* has always been served to recovering patients.

Sweat Induces Energy

The Korean expression, *yi-yeol-chi-yeol* means "fight fire with fire." Koreans savor steaming hot, spicy dishes such as *yukgaejang* in the belief that it helps them endure the heat of summer. The tender meat is easy to digest, and the spicy flavor wakes up the tired taste buds.

Originally, *yukgaejang* was a local dish of Seoul. In the early 1930s, Daeyeongwan, a restaurant located in Gongpyeong-dong, first began selling a soup loaded with scallions and very similar to the modern day *yukgaejang*. In Daegu, deemed to be the hottest region in Korea, they have a dish called *daegutang*, also a spicy beef soup. The word "*daegu*" in this case does not refer to the name of the city, but means "large dog."

The generous addition of scallions rids *yukgaejang* of any unpleasant smells from the animal fat. It's the perfect soup for summer.

Dakgaejang instead of *Yukgaejang*

Yukgaejang becomes *dakgaejang* when it is cooked with chicken in place of beef. The term *gaejang* in both names is derived from *gaejangguk* (spicy dog-meat soup). *Gaejangguk* was converted to *yukgaejang* when beef was used to replace dog meat, and *dakgaejang* when chicken was used.

Boknal

A *boknal* is one of the three hottest days of midsummer: *chobok*, *jungbok*, and *malbok*. These three days are collectively referred as *sambok*. The *boknals* are spaced at ten-day intervals during June and July of the lunar year. The heat during this season is called "*sambok-deowi*." In the Joseon royal court, the king granted his subjects "*bingpyo* (ice tickets)" with which they could draw ice from the royal icehouse. On *boknal*, *mineotang* (croaker soup), *samgyetang* (ginseng chicken soup), and *yukgaejang* were popular to restore physical stamina sapped by the hot weather.

The Good Luck Soup on New Year's Day
Tteok-guk
[Sliced Rice Cake Soup]

Tteok-guk is the traditional dish of Seolnal (Lunar New Year's Day). Korean people commonly use the expression "I ate a bowl of *tteok-guk*" to mean he or she has grown one year older. This soup is cooked in a broth made by simmering beef brisket or bones.

Hoping for Great Fortune

The custom of eating white rice cakes on New Year's Day originated from the ancient practice of worshiping the sun. The white color of the rice symbolizes the bright first day of a year, while the round form of the rice cake represents the orb of the sun. The long shape of *garaetteok* (cylindrical rice cake) also holds a special meaning: the long coils of the steamed *tteok* embodies the hope that one's wealth will grow in the same fashion, while the round profile of the sliced rice cakes symbolizes a round coin.

In the Gaeseong area, a northern region of Korea, there is a custom of eating *joraengi-tteokguk*. *Joraengi-tteok* is a three-centimeter-long white rice cake. With its pinched middle it looks like a gourd, but it is said that its shape was inspired by a silkworm. Since silkworms traditionally symbolized good luck, it appears to reflect the wish for good luck all year round.

Tteok-mandu-guk of the Colder Regions

There is another popular New Year's Day soup: *tteok-mandu-guk* (sliced rice cake soup with dumplings). *Tteok-mandu-guk* is made by adding *mandu* (dumplings) to the soup. Northerners make *mandu* the size of a baseball and add it to the rice cake soup. *Mandu* is not eaten very much in the warm southern regions. This could be because the ingredients, such as tofu or mung bean sprouts, can spoil easily. But it's more because *mandu* tastes so much better in cold weather. *Mandu* is a delight to eat, but also fun to make. In Korea, it was a long-held custom for family members to make *mandu* together to celebrate the New Year. As the old saying goes, "The best part of *songpyeon* (half-moon rice cake) is the skin, and the best part of *mandu* is the filling." The secret to tasty *mandu* is a generous amount of filling.

Fallen Snow in the Dining Room: *Garaetteok*
Rice flour is steamed in an earthen vessel and rolled into cylindrical pieces of *garaetteok*, from which regular ones are cut into coin-shaped slices for *tteokguk* and those smaller in diameter are used for *tteoksanjeok* (rice cake skewers), *tteokjjim* (braised rice cake), and *tteokbokki* (stir-fried rice cake).

A Hands-on Soup
Galbi-tang
[Short Rib Soup]

Galbi-tang is a soup made with beef ribs, sometimes called *gari-tang*. Ribs have always been one of the priciest beef cuts in Korea. The soup made from this expensive cut is, of course, a special treat and nourishing meal for anyone. *Galbi-tang* meal wouldn't be complete without taking the ribs with your hands and biting the succulent meat right off the bone.

Short Ribs, the Prime Cut

There are many nourishing dishes made by simmering meat or bones, but *galbi-tang* is the most sumptuous of them all. For these reasons, it became a favorite dish served to wedding guests. Traditionally, *galbi-tang* is cooked with only ribs, but the modern versions experiment with various ingredients and recipes. *Yeongyang-galbi-tang* (nutritious rib soup) is made by adding medicinal ingredients such as ginseng, jujubes, and pine nuts. *Wang-galbi-tang* (jumbo rib soup) is made with extra ribs for more meat-picking and finger-licking. Unlike ox leg bone soup or oxtail soup where water is continuously added to extract the flavor multiples of times, *galbi-tang* is only simmered until the meat is cooked just right.

Ugeoji-galbi-tang: A Popular Lunch Menu for Office Workers

Ugeoji-galbi-tang is soup made with green cabbage leaves and soybean paste in a short rib broth. It is popular as a hangover-soup as well as a lunch menu for office workers. *Ugeoji*, which refers to the boiled outer leaves of napa cabbage, is rich in vitamins, minerals and fiber and serves as the perfect dish for weight loss and skin care. The word "*ugeoji*" originated from the word "*utgeoji*," meaning "remove the top layer." When we see someone with a worried expression, we say "stop making an *ugeoji* face." But, a much friendlier *ugeoji*-comment would be "Hey, want to go grab a bowl of *ugeoji-galbi-tang*?"

Soy Sauce for *Galbi-tang*, Salt for *Seolleong-tang*
Galbi-tang and *seolleong-tang* differ in terms of the ingredients used to make the broth. While bones are used for *seolleong-tang*, the broth for *galbi-tang* gets its flavor from the meat on the ribs. Soup made from meat stocks like *galbi-tang* or *gomtang* (thick beef bone soup) tastes best when seasoned with soy sauce, while *seolleong-tang* tastes best when seasoned with salt.

Simmered Bone and Meat, All-in-one

Gomtang

[Thick Beef Bone Soup]

Gomtang is representative of Korean soup dishes along with *seolleong-tang* (ox bone soup). It combines the flavors of beef bone stock and boiled beef. *Gomtang* nourishes the body and soul with its high protein and calcium content.

The 125 Traditional Beef Cuts

The more cuts of beef used, the more savory the taste of *gomtang*. This is because the subtly different flavors of each cut fuse to produce a complex taste. Koreans are unrivalled when it comes to butchering the animal into intricate cuts. There are over 125 named cuts of beef such as *geollang, gogeori, godeulgae, gonjasoni, kkuri, dadae, dalgisal, daejeopsal, doraemokjeong, dungdeongi, ddeokshim, manhabatang, manhwa, myeokmire, balchae, saechang*, etc. This is a larger number compared to that of other countries, such as the Bodi tribe in East Africa which has 40 cuts, or the UK which has 25. The Koreans do not let any part of the animal go to waste: they even used to scrape off the gums for cooking.

Gom Means "Slow Simmer"

A Korean cookbook titled *Sieuijeonseo** describes *gomtang* as follows: "*Goeum* should be made by slow-simmering beef leg bones, shank, knuckles, tail, tripe, and chitterlings with abalone and sea cucumber, which are simmered in a generous amount of water over a low flame until the soup becomes thick and milky white." The word "*gom*" of *gomtang* means "soup made by slowly simmering meat or fish." It is an abbreviation of *goeum*, which originally meant "fatty food." By adding the suffix *tang* or *guk*, which mean simmered stew or soup, we arrive at *gomtang* or *gomguk* (another name for *gomtang*).

---

* *Sieuijeonseo* is an anonymous cookbook written at the end of 1800s. It recorded the traditional Korean food in the late Joseon Dynasty and is known as the first literature to mention *bibimbap*.

This thick soup, cooked by boiling down a meat broth over an extended period, is an excellent and nourishing dish with a wide variety of nutrients. As an easily digestible health food, it contains an anti-aging effect and is helpful for recovering from fatigue and preventing anemia.

A Local Specialty that Pleased the King
Seolleong-tang
[Ox Bone Soup]

Seolleong-tang is made by slow-simmering the cow's head, feet, meat, bones, and innards for hours. It is a popular lunch menu for office workers and tastes of the succulent and savory taste of beef. Add plenty of sliced scallions and eat it with *kkakdugi* (diced radish kimchi) for a nutritious one-dish meal.

Ttukbaegi, Scallion and *Kkakdugi*

In the late Joseon period, there were a number of famous *seolleong-tang* houses scattered around Seoul. At these spots, every part of the ox except the skin and a few byproducts would be immersed in a large cast iron pot and simmered from the early morning until one o' clock the next morning. The soup reaches a very thick stage by midnight. This is when the regular customers would start to flock to the restaurants.

Adding some tangy *kkakdugi* juice into the thick white soup is a fantastic combination and a great way to enjoy *seolleong-tang*. The taste of *seolleong-tang* is described in *Byeolgeongon*, a popular magazine from the 1920s: "A hearty soup is served in an earthen bowl with *kkakdugi*. Spoon in some scallion and red pepper flakes, season with salt and enjoy! Words cannot express the taste and nothing compares to the flavor. Even the pickiest eaters will not be able to resist *seolleong-tang*."

When you order a bowl of *seolleong-tang* at a restaurant, it will arrive almost instantly since it is simply ladled out of the pot into the bowl. No wonder the dish is a favorite among busy office workers.

Seonnongdan becomes *Seolleong-tang*

During the Joseon period, the most admired king in Korean history, King Sejong the Great, once performed a sacrificial rite at *seonnongdan* (the altar of agriculture) and ploughed the field as a demonstration to the people. Suddenly, a heavy rainstorm struck and the king was unable to return to the royal court. To relieve the king's hunger, the local people butchered an ox and served a soup made by boiling it in plain water. It is said that this later evolved to become *seolleong-tang*.

Gomtang vs. Seolleong-tang
In *Shikgaek* (The Gourmet), a popular Korean comic book, the difference between *gomtang* and *seolleong-tang* is summarized in a short sentence: "*Gomtang* is a meat soup whereas *seolleong-tang* is a bone soup." *Seolleong-tang* is milky white as the broth mainly comes from bones, whereas *gomtang* is clear as the broth mainly comes from meat.

A Restorative Food Harmonizing Chicken with Ginseng

Samgye-tang

[Ginseng Chicken Soup]

Samgye-tang is made by simmering a whole young chicken stuffed with ginseng, hedysarum root, jujubes, and sweet rice. Considered an energy-boosting dish best eaten during *sambok* (the hottest days of the lunar year), it is a classic Korean dish that has become popular among international diners as well.

A Must-eat Dish in the Summer

Samgye-tang is made by stuffing the cavity of a young chicken with sweet rice, ginseng, hedysarum root, and jujubes, trussing it and then simmering it in a stone pot or earthen bowl for about an hour. Sometimes, ground peanuts or perilla seeds are added for flavor and body. It became a popular dish once ginseng was made more widely available. The hot summer is the season for chicken. It is common in Korea for many restaurants which do not have *samgye-tang* on their menu to offer it in the hot summer season, which demonstrates the tremendous popularity of this soup.

Samgye-tang is well known to foreigners as well. Murakami Ryu, a renowned Japanese author, praised *samgye-tang* as the best Korean dish in his novel, while Zhang Yimou, a famous Chinese film director, said he enjoys it every time he visits Korea.

The Mother-in-law's *Samgye-tang*

Riding on the popularity of *samgye-tang*, "fusion *samgye-tang*" using unorthodox ingredients has become a growing trend. The new ingredients start with deer antler chips, chestnuts, and pine nuts and even include whole abalones (with shell) or whole red ginseng roots. There is the "Medicinal *samgye-tang*" seasoned with oriental medicinal herbs, the "Seafood *samgye-tang*" with baby octopus and blue crab, and the "Bamboo *samgye-tang*" that is served inside a hollow bamboo stalk. Regardless, nothing can beat the classic mother-in-law's homemade *samgye-tang*. In the old days, it was customary for a mother to kill one of her back-yard hens and prepare *samgye-tang* to welcome the son-in-law into her house. The mother-in-law's *samgye-tang* will always be special, because it was made with love and affection.

Ginseng
Attempts to trace the English word "ginseng" to its origin have been divided between two arguments. One is that it was derived from the Japanese pronunciation for the name of the plant, the other claims from the Chinese. However, it is today widely accepted that the word originated from the scientific name of the plant, "Panax ginseng," registered with the World Botanical Associates (WBA) by the Russian botanist Carl Anton von Meyer in 1843.

Fish Simmering in Spicy Red Chili Broth
Maeun-tang
[Spicy Fish Soup]

Maeun-tang refers to a fish stew with a spicy broth made of red pepper powder or paste. The whole fish is used to create a thicker broth, including the head and entrails. Although the stew can be prepared from both fresh and saltwater fish, freshwater fish such as catfish, mandarin fish, and yellow mandarin fish are considered to be best.

Freshwater Fish *Maeun-tang* for Taste and Stamina

Maeun-tang featuring freshwater fish grows tastier the longer it is simmered, as the plain broth becomes richer and thicker. Plenty of ground black pepper and ginger can be added to eliminate the fishy smell, while seasoning it with salt rather than soy sauce. Avid fans of freshwater *maeun-tang* will go fishing when the weather has cooled down and the crops have been harvested. This is the time when the fish are jumping, and in shallow spots where the water is clear and the riverbed is pebbled, fish buckets fill up quickly with the fresh catch. Freshly caught fish is simmered on the spot with summer squash, onions, green chili peppers, perilla leaves, crown daisy, and tofu in broth spiked with red chili paste.

Freshwater fish varies widely in size. Finger-sized fishes will fall off the bones after a while, at which point, chewy *sujebi* (korean pasta soup) or somen noodles should be added so that the broth thickens to a perfect consistency. A bowl of *maeun-tang* is filling and energizing. The addictive nature of the dish keeps the fans coming back to the river for more.

The Last Course in at *Hoe* Restaurants

Many Koreans always round off a meal of sliced raw fish (*hoe*) with spicy *maeun-tang*. So the final course at a *hoe* specialty restaurant is invariably a steaming bowl of spicy *maeun-tang* served with rice. While it is cooked quickly and the eating is without much gusto; nevertheless, the meal would not be complete without the last *maeun-tang* course. It would be like missing the dessert of a course meal.

Haemul-tang: The Delight of Mixed Seafood Flavors
The word "*haemul-tang*" is a compound of *haemul*, meaning seafood, with *tang*, soup. As the name indicates, it is a spicy stew made by boiling a wide variety of seafood, including fish, blue crab, baby octopus, shrimp, short-necked clams, and anything else that is in season. In short, the dish is a hodgepodge of ocean products. Seafood is rich in essential amino acids and taurine, which adds a deep and rustic flavor while combating adult diseases such as hypertension and heart disease.

Tender Meat that Falls off the Bone
Gamja-tang
[Pork Back-bone Stew]

Gamja-tang is made by simmering pork backbones with potatoes, green cabbage leaves, perilla seed powder, perilla leaves, scallions, and garlic. It is great fun to pick the meat off of the pork backbone. When the meat and potatoes are finished, a bowl of rice is added to the leftover broth and cooked for serving.

Pork Backbones and Whole Potatoes

Most people mistakenly believe that the soup is named after potatoes (*gamja*). But that is a misunderstanding. There are two main theories on the origin of the name. One is that the name refers to the marrow in the pork spine bone, which is also *gamja* in Korean. The other is that the name comes from the section of the pork backbone called *gamja*. There are also many different opinions as to the origin of the dish itself. Among them, the most plausible theory is as follows. When construction to build the railway between Seoul and Incheon started in 1899, a large number of workers flocked to Incheon harbor. These workers, who needed to keep up their strength, frequently ate a soup which was made of pork bones, potatoes, and dried radish leaves. Seeing this, a man named Han Dong-gil got the idea to open the first *gamja-tang* restaurant called "Hamba-jip" in 1900 in the Noryangjin area, where the final stage of construction of the Han River railway was underway.

A Cheap, Plentiful, and Nutritious Dish for All

Gamja-tang originated in the Jeolla Provinces. Since oxen were indispensible for farming, people cooked soup with pork instead of beef, by simmering vegetables in pork bone stock. This soup was fed to sick people or people suffering weak bones. Later, the soup spread to other regions and became a popular dish among commoners, especially the workers at Incheon harbor. *Gamja-tang* could enjoy such popularity due to several factors: it was a good accompaniment to drinking; it was a hearty food that filled the stomach; it was cheap in price but strong in flavor; and it was easy to prepare for large numbers of people.

As it became known that pork backbones were high in protein, calcium, and Vitamin B1, *gamja-tang*, a dish once relished by dockworkers, has become widely popular among Koreans regardless of age and occupation.

Perilla Seeds, Good for the Skin and Brain
Perilla seeds, an indispensable taste-enhancer in *gamja-tang*, are rich in Vitamins A and C which make the skin smooth and promotes brain functions. Thus, it has always been a part of the diet for brides-to-be and students.

JJIGAE & JEONGOL
[Stews and Hot Pots]

Jjigae is made by boiling a variety of ingredients together in a pot. It is seasoned and flavored with soybean paste *(doenjang)*, red chili paste *(gochujang)*, or dry-fermented soybeans *(cheonggukjang)*. *Jeongol* comprises of meat, vegetables, or other ingredients simmered at the table in a casserole pan, adding broth when necessary. *Jeongols* can simply consist of tofu or mushrooms, but also be prepared with meat, beef innards, *jeon* (pan-fried delicacies) or other elaborately prepared ingredients for a more colorful dish.

An Everyday Stew that's Hard to Resist
Doenjang-jjigae
[Soybean Paste Stew]

Doenjang (soybean paste) is an essential fermented condiment and a definitive ingredient of Korean cooking. This places *doenjang-jjigae* at the top of the list of dishes Koreans never tire of eating on a daily basis. An earthenware bowl of bubbling hot *doenjang-jjigae* is the perennial soul food that reminds Koreans of home and family.

Doenjang-jjigae: The Joy of Simplicity

The taste and name of *doenjang* differ according to the characteristics and conditions of the region, such as *makdoenjang, tojang, makjang, damppukjang, jeupjang, saenghwaljang, cheongtaejang, patjang, dubujang, jiryejang, saengchijang, bijijang, mujang, jinyangdoenjang, miryangdoenjang, jejudo-jopijang*, and countless more. While *doenjang* is undoubtedly a uniquely Korean product, similar soybean pastes are found in neighboring countries such as the Japanese *miso* or the Chinese *huángjiàng* or *dòujiàng* (or *tauchu*). In the old days, people fermented their own *doenjang* at home. Now, the vast majority buy commercially manufactured products. But homemade and store-bought *doenjangs* must be cooked differently in order to bring out the desired flavor. Homemade *doenjang* tends to have a stronger, richer flavor, and has to be cooked slowly over low heat. Mass-produced *doenjang*, however, tastes best when boiled rapidly over high heat, because overcooking will give the *jjigae* an acidic taste and much of the flavor will be lost. Cooking time is proportionate to how long the *doenjang* was aged; the more mature the *doenjang*, the longer it should be cooked.

Gangdoenjang-jjigae: A Late-summer Dish

A pot of thick, chunky *gangdoenjang-jjigae* is a versatile dish. It is made with minced meat or anchovies, crushed garlic, chopped scallion, sesame oil, and *doenjang* which are boiled in *ssaltteumul* (water left over from rinsing rice). It is the ultimate summertime dish to accompany a bowl of rice. Another summertime favorite is *gangdoenjang-bibimbap*, which is rice mixed with a spoonful of *gangdoenjang* stew, young radish kimchi, and sesame oil.

The Simple Process of Making *Doenjang*
In late autumn, soybeans are boiled, compressed into blocks called *meju*, and hung to dry for the winter. This dried *meju* becomes the base ingredient for *doenjang*. In early spring, the *meju* is placed in a crock, which is then filled with brine, and after approximately one hundred days, the remaining solids are separated from the liquid, mashed into a paste and stored in a separate crock to ripen into scrumptious *doenjang*. The dark remaining liquid is aged separately to create soy sauce.

Pork Chunks Round Off the Taste
Kimchi-jjigae
[Kimchi Stew]

One of the most beloved lunch menu for Korean office workers is *kimchi-jjigae*. It is a safe choice at any restaurant, never disappoints, and is always served in generous portions. The same is true at home. All you need is sour, fully-ripe kimchi and water. Pork and anchovies are the two most favorite ingredients added to enhance the flavor of *kimchi-jjigae*.

Pork, Anchovies, Tuna, or Mackerel

Along with kimchi fried rice, *kimchi-jjigae* is one of the best ways to use up sour kimchi. Even a small addition of pork, tuna, mackerel or anchovies neutralizes the sourness of kimchi, and tastes unbelievably good with rice. Recently, *mugeunji*, or aged kimchi, has been gaining popularity. When kimchi is matured at low temperatures for over six months, it becomes *mugeunji*, which is less sour and sports a stronger fermented flavor. Boiling *mugeunji* with large chunks of pork or a generous portion of mackerel or mackerel pike turns it into a "rice thief," because the resulting *jjigae* is so delicious that rice literally seems to disappear in plain sight. Adding *doenjang* or *gochujang* to *dongchimi* (radish water kimchi), *kkakdugi* (diced radish kimchi) or leftover kimchi will intensify the flavor, while adding pork chunks or pork ribs instead of anchovies results in a nutritious and hearty dish suited for winter.

How to Make a Delicious *Kimchi-jjigae*

Boiling kimchi in water from the start leaves it soggy, depriving the interesting crunchy texture of the napa cabbage. One must first stir-fry the kimchi in a small amount of oil over high heat, add water when the kimchi has turned soft, lower the heat, and then leave it to simmer until the desired consistency. This is the secret behind a rich broth and crunchy kimchi pieces. The *jjigae* may be seasoned with fresh kimchi liquid instead of salt for an even more intense flavor.

A Long-awaited Delicacy: *Mugeunji*
Aged kimchi is known as *mugeunji* when it has ripened over a long period but not grown sour. *Mugeunji* is used for making *jjigae* when it has matured for a shorter period and for making *ssam* or *jjim*, after being lightly washed, when it has been aged for longer periods. The deeper its flavor grows as it ages in buried earthenware crocks, the more fantastic *mugeunji* dish will taste.

Pungent but Delicious
Cheongguk-jang-jjigae
[Rich Soybean Paste Stew]

Cheongguk-jang-jjigae is stew made by boiling beef, tofu, kimchi, and other ingredients in water together with a *cheongguk-jang* (dry-fermented soybeans). Using the water left over from rinsing rice instead of plain water helps minimize any unappetizing smells and brings out the mouth-watering flavor. *Cheongguk-jang* is enjoyed throughout the nation, but it is especially popular in North Chungcheong, Jeolla, and Gyeongsang Provinces.

Soybeans Fermented with Rice Straw

Cheongguk-jang is a special type of soybean paste prepared by fermenting boiled soybeans in a warm room. Despite the similarity in appearance, *cheongguk-jang* is completely different from the Japanese *natto*. While *natto* is usually made by artificially inoculating bacteria, *cheongguk-jang* develops through a natural process of fermentation or with microorganisms drawn from rice straw. In the past, *cheongguk-jang* blocks used to be fermented for a longer time to create a more pungent paste, but today, less odorous products are more popular. It is not that difficult to make *cheongguk-jang*: boiled soybeans are placed in an earthenware container, covered with rice straw, and stored in a warm room while the bacteria Bacillus subtilis propagates, creating a thick liquid. When the fermentation is complete, minced garlic and ginger, coarsely ground red chili peppers, salt and other spices are added. It is then crushed into a coarse paste and stored in the refrigerator. The necessary amount can be spooned out any time you feel hungry for *cheongguk-jang-jjigae*.

Originally Fermented Under a Saddle

Because *cheongguk* is the term for Qing Dynasty in the Korean language, many people tend to believe *cheongguk-jang* was introduced from China. In truth, it is a uniquely Korean condiment that was invented in Goguryeo, an ancient Korean kingdom. It is said to have been first produced by the people of Goguryeo, as they kept boiled soybeans underneath their horse saddles when crossing Manchuria and removed handfuls whenever they were hungry. Due to the horse's body heat (37 to 40°C), the beans would undergo a natural fermentation process and transformed into a nutritious paste that could be stored for extended periods. The constant temperature maintained between the saddle and horse turned out to be ideal for making *cheongguk-jang*.

More Than Food

In every ten grams of *cheongguk-jang*, there are roughly thirty billion beneficial microorganism which, once consumed, act as a natural digestive aid by making their way to the intestines and aiding bowel functions. Bacillus subtilis, the bacteria responsible for the sticky strings found in *cheongguk-jang*, is one hundred times better at aiding digestion than is Lactobacillus. *Cheongguk-jang* also contains thrombolytic enzymes that decompose protein, and therefore helps ward off heart diseases and strokes. *Cheongguk-jang* is great in *jjigae*, but it is even healthier when consumed uncooked. To offset the pungent smell, *cheongguk-jang* can be eaten wrapped in dried laver or kimchi.

Simmering Stew in Earthenware
Sundubu-jjigae
[Soft Tofu Stew]

A pot of *sundubu-jjigae* fresh from the stove is a mouth-watering sight. The bubbling sound of the stew, seemingly about to boil over the rim, stimulates the taste buds. A spoonful of *saeujeot* (salted shrimp) is the perfect seasoning for a mild *sundubu-jjigae* made from silky smooth *sundubu* (soft tofu). As for the spicy version, nothing beats the taste of a raw egg cracked into the pot and eaten with bits of meat and seafood.

Sundubu: The Best Source of Soybean Nutrients

Sundubu starts out being made in the same manner as ordinary tofu, first boiling soymilk then coagulating it by adding a little brine. But it skips the later steps of draining and pressing the lumpy bean curds. The silky texture makes this lightly flavored delicacy easy to digest. The key to producing delicious *sundubu* lies in using the proper type of brine. A village famous for its *sundubu*, Chodang Village uses clean water from the East Sea. It all started when Chodang Heoyeop, a civil official of the mid-sixteenth-century Joseon government, was appointed as the magistrate of Gangneung. He discovered that the water from a spring in the front yard of his office tasted so good that he made tofu from the spring water and used sea water instead of brine. The name "Chodang" was adopted from Heoyeop's pen name. *Chodang sundubu* calls for a labor-intensive process with only a small output, but long-standing restaurants still insist on preparing their own *sundubu* in this traditional way. Sometimes, *sundubu* is served plain and hot with a soy sauce mixture on the side for seasoning, but it is also delicious when boiled together with sour kimchi or seafood such as oysters or clams.

Praised by the *New York Times*

An article in the *New York Times* featuring tofu dishes attracted great attention in Korea when it praised *sundubu-jjigae* as "the ideal winter meal." Featuring a picture of *sundubu-jjigae*, the review of tofu restaurants in Manhattan included Book Chang Dong, Cho Dang Gol, Li Hua, and Seoul Garden. The article described *sundubu-jjigae* as "a hearty brew of spicy broth and silken tofu that is served in cast-iron bowls. Topped with scallion and nuggets of tender oxtail or crisp kimchi, it's the ideal winter meal."

No Need to Add Water
Sundubu-jjigae can be made without any adding broth or water since the *sundubu* itself releases water when boiled. In an earthenware bowl, place minced pork fat, *sundubu*, seasoning paste, shelled and drained clams in that order and boil over high heat. It is essential to continue stirring while it boils to keep the *sundubu* from burning.

A Tasty Mix of Ham, Sausage, and Kimchi
Budae-jjigae
[Sausage Stew]

First created during the Korean War, *budae-jjigae* has a relatively short history. Kimchi and *gochujang* (red chili paste) are mixed into a broth and boiled with bits of ham, sausage, and baked beans to create this spicy "army base stew." The stew, despite its names, was enjoyed not by the GIs living on the US Army bases but by those residing in the surrounding areas.

Born in the City of Uijeongbu

In the depths of the Korean War, it was relatively easy to find sausage or ham near US Army bases. When such preserved meats, collectively known as "army base meat," were boiled in a *gochujang* broth together with kimchi, the displeasing taste of the excessive fat was minimized and a rather tasty meal could be had. Also dubbed "*jonseun-tang*" (Johnson Stew) after the U.S. president, Lyndon B. Johnson, *budae-jjigae* is a good example of the Koreans' particular fondness for spicy broths. When people first tasted ham and sausage, they were fascinated by the taste of these meat products that was so unlike any meat they had ever experienced, but they still found them to be somewhat lacking as an accompaniment to steamed rice. After much painstaking effort, a technique was developed to convert them into a piquant stew, and the rest is history. It is said that *budae-jjigae* started out as a buttery stir-fried snack of sausage, ham, cabbage, and onions to accompany *makgeolli* (Korean rice wine), but later on, *gochujang*, kimchi, and broth were added to create the taste that is cherished today.

Uijeongbu *Budae-jjigae* Alley
The birthplace of the original *budae-jjigae* was Uijeongbu, a city defined by its US Army base. One after another, *budae-jjigae* restaurants opened and created what is today known as the Uijeongbu *Budae-jjigae* Alley. Nowadays, the alley has become a tourist spot that even attracts foreign visitors to Uijeongbu.

A Court Dish of Regal Splendor
Sinseollo
[Royal Hot Pot]

Originally consumed only in the royal palace, *sinseollo* was so lavish that it also became known as *yeolguja-tang*, or "a stew that enchants the mouth." There are roughly 25 principle luxury ingredients in *sinseollo*, including beef, beef liver and tripe, pork, pheasant and chicken meat, abalone, sea cucumber and gray mullet.

The Meal of a Vagabond

The origins of *sinseollo* trace back to the reign of King Yeonsangun in 15th century Joseon. A man talented in poetry and prose, and knowledgeable in the nature of *yin* and *yang*, who went by the name of Jeong Hui-ryang, cast his own fortune. Aware of his fate and the moment of his own death, he decided one day to renounce the secular world and live the rest of his live in seclusion. After falling on the wrong side of the king and being forced to live in exile, Jeong left to reside deep in the forests, but is said to have wandered the peninsula like a *sinseon*, or a Tao Immortal. Wherever he went, Jeong carried a brazier he had made himself and cooked a blend of vegetables in it all together. When he left the world to become an actual *sinseon*, people began to call his brazier *sinseollo*.

A Stew that Enchants the Mouth

As lavish as the ingredients required to make *sinseollo* are, preparing the dish is a similarly elaborate task. First, lay out the slices of raw and boiled meat at the bottom of the brazier and spread an evenly-proportioned layer of various *jeon* (bite-sized meat or vegetables pan-fried in egg batter) made from fish, beef, pork, *cheonyeop*,* Korean parsley, eggs, and mushrooms. Pine nuts, walnuts, and ginkgo nuts are sprinkled on top to complete it, and then a broth is poured over the entire preparation and boiled on the spot. In the center of the *sinseollo* pan is a round cylindrical compartment, where glowing charcoal is placed to cook the ingredients and keep the food at the proper temperature.

Cheonyeop (omasum) is the third stomach of ruminant animals such as cattle, sheep or deer, which is consumed raw, as fresh slices dipped in sesame oil and salt, or pan-fried in egg batter as *cheonyeop-jeon*, either separately or as an ingredient for a *jeongol* hotpot.

Sinseollo and State Banquets
With its visually pleasing and colorful arrangement, *sinseollo* is a favorite menu for state banquets. The former First Lady of the Republic of Korea, Kim Yoon-ok is said to have dimmed the lights during a state banquet to serve *sinseollo* because the floating procession of *sinseollo* pots, each glowing red with a burning piece of charcoal, in itself served as a visual performance.

Chewy Beef Chitterlings in a Hot Spicy Broth
Gopchang-jeongol
[Beef Tripe Hot Pot]

Jeongol is a hotpot of seasoned bits of meat and a blend of vegetables, consumed as it boils while continuously topping it up with broth to prevent it from boiling dry. Among the many different *jeongols*, the type with beef chitterlings, or *gopchang-jeongol*, is considered the best. When the weather turns cold, many Koreans' thoughts turn to sharing a hot and spicy pot of *gopchang-jeongol* seasoned with a generous scoop of red chili powder.

A Gourmet Dish Made with Beef Chitterlings

Gopchang is the sometimes odorous small intestines of cattle. Because of the high fat content, coiled shape and wooly villi lining the insides, *gopchang* is not a simple ingredient to prepare for cooking. Strangely, once cooked, it satisfies the palate with its chewy texture and buttery taste. *Gopchang* is ideal either boiled in a *jeongol* or grilled. High in protein, *gopchang* is known to be a healthy food that protects the stomach's lining and breaks down alcohol. The enzymes found inside the *gopchang* aid digestion. It may appear to be overly greasy, but *gopchang* is actually easy to digest and can be consumed even by those in poor health. While the high price prevents most people from enjoying it on a daily basis, a boiling *jeongol* of well-prepared *gopchang* is ideal for special occasions or family gatherings. A rich broth is essential for a proper *gopchang-jeongol*, and light soy sauce for soup is always added for flavor. The addition of fragrant crown daisy leaves right before serving helps cleanse and refresh the palate.

A Fatty yet Savory Meat

The outer surface of *gopchang* is covered with a considerable layer of fat. This fat has to be removed to get rid of the gamy taste and allow the full enjoyment of *gopchang's* flavor. The best way to purge the unwanted odor is to use flour. After the fat is removed, *gopchang* should be scrubbed with flour and the odor will vanish.

As a high-protein/low-cholesterol food, beef tripe protects the stomach lining, breaks down alcohol and promotes digestion, making it a suitable accompaniment to alcohol and an especially efficacious food for post-partum recovery.

Noodles Served in Simmering Broth
Guksu-jeongol
[Noodle Hot Pot]

Guksu-jeongol literally means "hotpot with noodles," meaning that the main ingredient is noodles. Beef, mushrooms, assorted vegetables, and noodles are all boiled in a broth extracted from dried anchovies or dried kelp to create this relatively affordable and therefore popular *jeongol*.

A Simple yet Hearty *Jeongol*

Surprisingly, most people never attempt at preparing *jeongol* because they think that it's too difficult to make at home. Depending on how one looks at it, however, there are few dishes simpler to prepare than *jeongol*. If you want to enjoy something bubbling hot, there is no need to dine out; just open your refrigerator. Simply fill a casserole pan with plenty of mushrooms and leftover bits of carrot and onion, and you will have a hearty broth. *Guksu-jeongol*, in particular, is a low-budget meal. Normally with a *jeongol*, the meat and vegetable bits are eaten first, leaving a rich broth still simmering in the pan. Only then are the noodles cooked in the broth and consumed. In *guksu-jeongol*, however, a generous portion of noodles are cooked from the very beginning. *Myeon-sinseollo* (royal noodle hotpot), was a traditional dish that resembles today's *guksu-jeongol*. It appears in *Jinchanuigwe*,* published in 1868, and is recorded as "pieces of beef, sea cucumber, shrimp, clam, thin scallions, Korean parsley (*minari*), and bamboo shoots placed in a circle and boiled with wheat noodles in a broth." This shows that *jeongol* doesn't necessarily have to be lavish with toppings such as meat or pan-fried fish. By featuring noodles as the central ingredient, it can become a very frugal and humble dish.

The flavor of *jeongol* hinges on the meat broth. However, seafood such as squid or blue crabs can take the place of beef. *Jeongol* can be cooked with ease once the main ingredients have been selected from among meat, seafood, or mushrooms, along with vegetables as essential side ingredients to dip and boil together.

**Jinchanuigwe* is a record for royal court birthday banquet of the king, queen, and queen dowager in the late Joseon Dynasty.

The Origin of the *Jeongol* Pan
The casserole pan used for making *jeongol* was also called *beonggeojitgol* or *gamtugol* because it looked like an upside-down soldier's hat (*beonggeoji*) or official's hat (*gamtu*). The form is said to have been derived from ancient times when soldiers, who did not have proper tools for cooking during campaigns, would flip their helmets (*jeollip*) upside down and cook food in them.

An Excellent Source of Nutrition
Dubu-jeongol
[Tofu Hot Pot]

Originally, *dubu-jeongol* was only consumed in the royal court. Flat squares of tofu are pan-fried until yellow. Then, a thin slice of beef seasoned with various spices is sandwiched between two squares of tofu, and tied with a strand of thin scallion like a small wrapped gift. These tofu sandwiches and sliced vegetables are arranged in a circle in a pot, topped with garnish and simmered.

Tofu: One of the Most Ingenious Human Inventions

Bean curd, better known by its Japanese name "tofu," was first made in ancient China. It spread to Japan via Korea, and then to most parts of East Asia. Wherever Buddhism and its emphasis on vegetarianism prevailed, so did tofu. There are three main theories about the origins of tofu. The first suggests that it was initially an accidental creation of Líu Ān, King of Hunainan in northern China around BC 164, during the Han Dynasty, when he was making soy milk for a sick mother who could no longer chew whole soybeans. The second version claims that sea salt was accidentally spilled into a boiling pot of ground soybeans. It says that as soon as sea salt, which contains calcium and magnesium, both necessary for tofu coagulation, dropped into the boiling soybean liquid, it caused the liquid to congeal into a firmer gel, and thereby gave birth to tofu. This theory is plausible because ancient literature also records that soybean was used to make stews. The third theory states that the ancient Chinese drew upon the cheese-making methods of the Mongols. While there is no evidence of how such techniques propagated to ancient China, this theory is based on the similarity between the Chinese words for Mongolian fermented milk, *rufu* and, *doufu* (tofu). In the West there is cheese, and in the East we have soft and savory tofu. However, tofu is considered a healthier food because unlike cheese, an animal product high in fat, tofu is high in protein and low in calories and fat.

Tofu is made from soybeans, sometimes called the "beef from the fields." High in protein and low in calories, soybeans are good for health. Eat as much as you want without worrying about developing lifestyle diseases.

A Nutritous, Healthy Hotpot
Mandu-jeongol
[Dumplings Hot Pot]

When it has gotten chilly in the morning and evening, it is the season for *jeongol*. *Mandu-jeongol* is served in generous portions, with plenty of *mandu* (dumplings) in each bowl. It is a highly nutritious and filling meal. Add meat *mandu* for a milder taste, or kimchi *mandu* for a spicy version of this versatile hotpot.

A Winter Dish that Fills the Stomach and Soul

There is probably no dish that is as satisfying as a casserole of *mandu-jeongol*: it satisfies both the eyes and the stomach. Even if individual portions are smaller compared to steamed *mandu* or *tteok-mandu-guk* (rice cake soup with dumplings), everyone ends up feeling full and happy at the end of a meal of *mandu-jeongol*. It's also a good accompaniment to alcoholic drinks. As our ancestors would sometimes eat *mandu* instead of rice, *mandu-jeongol* doesn't need rice to serve as a full meal. In fact, few dishes are easier to prepare than *mandu-jeongol*, because the *mandu* can be made at home but store-bought is also easily available. If you prefer a lighter taste, boil meat *mandu* in a clear broth, but for a spicier version, kimchi *mandu* can be boiled with an addition of chili powder or chopped extra-hot *cheongyang* peppers to the broth.

A Well-balanced Dish

Mung bean sprouts in *mandu* filling detoxify the body, reduce fever, and stimulate the appetite. In addition, the bean curd in the filling contains plenty of calcium, playing a major role in maintaining healthy bones and teeth. As a result, *mandu* hotpot, with its wide variety of ingredients in the filling, is an excellent food in terms of nutritional balance.

If you find the broth a bit too oily, red pepper flakes can be added to bring out a more refreshing taste. In addition, *memil-guksu* (buckwheat noodles) as a side ingredient can provide a flavor quite distinct from that of wheat flour noodles.

A Harmonious Blend of Sweet *Bulgogi* and Spicy Baby Octopus

Bullak-jeongol

[***Bulgogi*** and Octopus Hot Pot]

It is difficult to describe the taste of *bullak-jeongol* in one sentence, because the sweetness of *bulgogi* and the robust spices used to season the *nakji* (baby octopus) are married to create a novel gastronomic experience. It starts spicy, but ends with a clear note. Combining the ingredients is complex, but when successfully performed, the end result is a fantastic harmony of flavors.

Nakji: *Ginseng* of the Sea

Nakji is loaded with protein and healthy minerals, and is as energizing as beef. Rich in DHA and taurine, *nakji* is also great for brain development and overcoming fatigue. In his record of marine life, *Jasaneobo*,* the Joseon scholar Jeong Yak-jeon writes of how an ox that had passed out from heatstroke were fed *nakji* to be set back on their feet. Even to this day in the south, whenever cattle collapse after giving birth or from heatstroke, they are offered a large *nakji*. As soon as it swallows the *nakji*, the ox was reported to stand up right on the spot. Aside from the validity of this report, it is not uncommon to see owners coil up a whole *nakji* and feed it to their fighting bulls.

* *Jasaneobo* is the oldest surviving record of marine life in Korea, completed in 1814 by the Joseon scholar Jeong Yak-jeon, who personally collected, studied and recorded the names, appearances, behaviors, usages, of more than 155 different species of marine life from the coastal waters surrounding Heuksan Island, South Jeolla Province.

Thin and Refreshing *Yeonpo-tang*
Yeonpo-tang is a clear broth made with small octopus and vegetables. People living on the West Coast of Korea prefer *yeonpo-tang*, with its refreshing taste, to fiery *nakji-bokkeum* (sautéed octopus). More suitable for *yeonpo-tang* are medium-sized octopus, rather than smaller ones. Sometimes the soup may turn black if an ink sac accidentally pops, which is part of the fun of eating *yeonpo-tang*.

JJIM, JORIM & BOKKEUM

[Braised Dishes, Glazed Dishes and Stir-fried Dishes]

The Korean cuisine is healthy because it tends to use braising and simmering rather than deep-frying or grilling. This will dissolve extra fat in the ingredient and minimize the total fat content. Braising, simmering over low heat for a long time, and stir-frying with a minimal amount of oil allow one to add vegetables and spices and bring out the flavors of ingredients.

The Quintessential Holiday Food
Galbi-jjim
[Braised Short Ribs]

Galbi-jjim was mostly served on birthdays or holidays, because it is made from the choicest and most expensive beef part. Indeed, *galbi-jjim* always reminds people of special occasions or holidays, when family members are brought together.

Sweet and Tender Short Ribs

Korean cooking consists of a large number of braised dishes that require considerable culinary skill. *Galbi-jjim* is one such dish, growing in popularity among international diners who appreciate the health advantages of braised dishes. When making *galbi-jjim*, the fat on the short ribs is carefully removed before braising. Carrots, ginkgo nuts, and chestnuts are added, and finally shiitake and egg garnish are sprinkled on top to complete the cooking process. Internatinonally, this dish is becoming as popular as *galbi-gui* (grilled marinated short ribs). Glazed with soy sauce and topped with ginkgo nuts and chestnuts, *galbi-jjim* looks and tastes wonderful. *Satae-jorim* (braised beef shanks), which uses beef shanks in the place of fattier short ribs, is also popular due to its leaner taste.

Hot and Spicy *Jjim-galbi*

Jjim-galbi (steamed short ribs), which tastes completely different from traditional *galbi-jjim*, is said to have originated in an alley in Dongin-dong, Daegu in the 1960s. According to one story, a married couple who greatly enjoyed short ribs used to steam them in an iron pot and eat them with salt. Gradually they added more and more garlic and hot peppers to suit the husband's passion for spicy food. After a while, the wife developed a special hot sauce and began to sell short ribs steamed in the sauce out of a small traditional house. It was an instant hit among the residents of Daegu, who have a love for extra spicy food. Other restaurants selling the dish quickly sprouted up along the same row, which is today known as "*Jjim-galbi* Alley."

The Secret of Dongin-dong *Jjim-galbi*
The famous *jjim-galbi* restaurant in Dongin-dong uses nickel silver pots in order to quickly steam short ribs for *jjim-galbi*. The ribs are served with lettuce and perilla leaves, and sometimes wrapped in *baek-kimchi* (white kimchi) to temper the spiciness. After finishing all the meat from the pot, many diners like to mix rice with the remaining sauce. It is near impossible to find an undented or unbruised cooking pot in Dongin-dong restaurants. This is because of the practice of crowding multiple pots over a briquette fire.

Reminiscing *Dakdori-tang*
Dak-maeun-jjim
[Braised Chili Chicken]

Dak-maeun-jjim is made with cut-up chicken, onions, potatoes, and other vegetables, which are marinated in a spicy sauce and braised together. The dish can be made with less liquid to be less sloppy and presentable to guests. But, most people prefer the country-style version, which boils the ingredients in plenty of liquid to create a thick, bubbling sauce.

Dakdori-tang, the Ongoing Debate

Dak-maeun-jjim is still called *dakdori-tang* by many. Following a long, fierce debate, the official name of the dish was changed from *dakdori-tang* to *dak-bokkeum-tang* and finally to the current term. It all started when the National Institute of Korean Language issued an opinion that the name should be changed, because the *dori* in *dak-dori-tang* is the Japanese word for bird. From that point, the dish was officially known as *dak-bokkeum-tang,* which led to complaints from those accustomed to the original name saying that the new name did not sound appetizing. It can be likened to the once questionable renaming of "French fries" to the far less appealing "Freedom Fries." One argument recently gaining support is that *dakdori-tang* is a legitimate Korean term, because *dori* was not derived from Japanese but rather from the Korean verb, *dorida* (to cut out). By whatever name it may be called, the tender chicken pieces and potatoes braised in a spicy sauce which is later mixed with rice, is an all-time favorite among Koreans.

Dak-maeun-jjim Broth

Home-cooked *dak-maeun-jjim* is not cooked with a lot of broth, but the restaurant version tends to have an ample amount of broth, because the dish has to be continuely simmered at the table. Sometimes, a large amount of potato chunks are added. Once cooked, the potatoes are mashed with spoons and eaten with the hot broth. *Buldak* (hotand spicy chicken), which includes extra hot *cheongyang* red peppers, is a version where the chicken is stir-fried without broth on a hot pan. Those who love spicy food enjoy *buldak* for its tongue-paralyzing, head-spinning spiciness.

Andong-jjimdak, A Sweet Taste from Soy Sauce
Andong-style braised chicken *andong-jjimdak* is not red, but dark brown from being cooked in soy sauce. Still, the dish packs enough spice to bring sweat to most brows. The spiciness comes from the extra hot *cheongyang* red pepper. Many believe that *andong-jjimdak* originated from a prestigious family from the Andong region, but it was actually invented in the chicken alley of the so-called Old Andong Market in the late 1970s as an affordable yet generous dish to be shared among a large group.

To Revive a Tired Body
Dak-baeksuk
[Whole Chicken Soup]

One of the most popular foods to help alleviate the heat of summer is *dak-baeksuk*. On hot days, the father will say, "How about boiling a chicken today?" Come evening, and there it would be on the table: *dak-baeksuk*, a nourishing dish with plenty of garlic and sweet rice. Oftentimes, a mother will serve *dak-baeksuk* even in winter, if she sees that the family members could use some sprucing up.

A Dish for Cooling the Heat

During the hot summer, our ancestors used to choose a date and collect money for an excursion to a nearby valley creek. The purpose was to get away from the heat, relax, and eat something nutritious. After soaking their feet in the cool valley stream, they sat under a shady tree to enjoy steaming *dak-baeksuk* boiled in a large pot. They consumed the chicken meat with sea salt, and afterwards poured soaked sweet rice into the soup to make rice porridge. While a spring chicken, also known as a medicinal chicken, was considered ideal for *dak-baeksuk*, meaty roosters were sometimes cooked for large gatherings. The tradition of eating *dak-baeksuk* at valley creeks in the peak of summer still remains; today, numbers of *dak-baeksuk* restaurants populate resort spots in mountain valleys.

Nurungji-baeksuk, Savory and Chewy Delicacy

One of the popular modern variations of *baeksuk* is *hanbang-baeksuk* (medicinal whole chicken soup), prepared with traditional medicinal ingredients such as dried jujubes, chestnuts, and milk vetch roots. Equally popular is the *nurungji-baeksuk* (scorched rice and whole chicken soup). Unlike the regular *dak-baeksuk*, where sweet rice is added to the remaining broth, the *nurungji-baeksuk* starts out with covering the bottom of the pressure cooker with soaked sweet rice. The sweet rice layer absorbs the chicken stock while it cooks, and becomes slightly burnt with a chewy texture and wonderful flavor.

Differences between *Dak-baeksuk* and *Samgye-tang*
Samgye-tang is a chicken boiled with a variety of medicinal ingredients such as ginseng, hedysarum roots, chestnuts, and ginkgo nuts, together with glutinous rice. Meanwhile, *dak-baeksuk* is chicken boiled in simple plain water, with no medicinal ingredients added, then the broth being used to cook *juk* (rice porridge).

Non-greasy, Succulent Boiled Pork

Bossam

[Napa Wraps with Pork]

The pork in *bossam* is boiled in a way that eliminates any unpleasant odor, and then placed under a heavy stone to squeeze out oily fat from the meat. The defatted meat is sliced and eaten with lettuce or napa cabbage leaves. The meat is dipped in salted shrimp sauce (*saeu-jeot*) and wrapped in yellow cabbage leaves with a spicy mix of white radish and chestnuts.

Pork, for Natural Detoxification

Pork is ideal for ridding the body of toxic substances such as lead or mercury. Because its melting point is below human body temperature, pork fat assists in drawing out toxins that the human body absorbed from the polluted air or water. Pork fat is said to be effective for the prevention of pneumoconiosis, or "black lung," which can be caused by breathing in soot or dust. Perhaps this is why miners and construction workers always eat pork at gatherings to scrub the dirt from the throat. Pork contains five to ten times more B vitamins than beef, and is rich in high-quality proteins and other nutrients. Also, the iron in pork has high absorption efficiency and helps to prevent iron deficiency anemia.

Healthy Meals for a Long Life

It is healthier to consume pork steamed, as in *bossam*, than grilled. In Okinawa, the southern Japanese island famous for longevity, the numerous centenarians enjoy steamed pork simmered in soy sauce. Many long-lived Korean elders also mention steamed pork as one of their favorite foods.

Suyuk, **Boiled and Sliced Meat**
Suyuk refers to sliced, boiled, and pressed meat. Usually *suyuk* refers to boiled beef, while *jeyuk* refers to boiled pork. Beef *suyuk* is dipped in vinegared soy sauce or mustard soy sauce, while pork *suyuk* is dipped in salted shrimp sauce and wrapped in kimchi. The latter is a perfect combination, since the kimchi and shrimp sauce include enzymes that break down pork fat which otherwise may not digest well.

A Classic Late-night Snack
Jokbal
[Pigs' Feet]

Jokbal with salted shrimp sauce wrapped in lettuce leaves is one of the most preferred dishes to accompany wine or spirits. It is also popular as a late-night snack. Although *jokbal* is made with pork, the texture is unique. Its firm texture comes from the gelatin content of the skin and cartilage.

Jokbal, Loved for the texture and flavor

The word *jokbal* automatically conjures up images of Jangchung-dong, a Seoul neighborhood street lined with *jokbal* places. Starting about 40 years ago, these restaurants opened one by one until they finally formed a sprawling cluster. Curiously, almost all of these restaurants claim to be the first or "the original" one, as indicated in their signs. *Jokbal* is believed to have been invented by Yi Gyeong-seon, a seasoned Jangchung-dong restauranter who arrived in Seoul after fleeing from the North during the Korean War. Yi took the pork trotter dish from her hometown and added traditional Chinese five-spice to it. Displaced Northerners saw the sign "Pyeongan Province *Jokbal*" and flocked to her restaurant. Then came the crowds from nearby Jangchung Stadium and National Theater. The restaurant's great success created what is called the *jokbal* Street. These days, *jokbal* has also become popular among women who heard about its benefits on the skin. A substance called chondroitin, plentiful in *jokbal*, is a bioactive substance that slows down the aging process. In China, pig trotters are a popular birthday dish along with noodles, as the two symbolize health and longevity. The resemblance between *jokbal* and the German dish "*Eisbein*," ham hock boiled in beer, is also quite remarkable.

Jokbal for New Mothers

Jokbal promotes the secretion of breast milk, and the protein from the pork trotters enhances the quality of the breast milk. In the past, new mothers who had trouble breastfeeding, used to drink the broth of simmered pork trotters. However, due to the complexity of the process and the unpleasant smell of the broth, modern-day mothers opt for *jokbal* instead.

Jokpyeon, a Dish for Royalties

Jokpyeon (jellied ox feet) is another traditional dish that also makes good use of gelatin. To create *jokpyeon*, beef shanks are boiled with chicken or pheasant, and the meat is removed, chopped, and then put back in the broth. This is topped with red chili pepper threads, slices of boiled egg, and sautéed stone ear mushrooms and cooled until the gelatin sets. *Jokpyeon* requires an elaborate process and was mostly prepared in the royal court where it was appreciated for for the visual effect.

The Transformation of an Ugly Fish
Agwi-jjim
[Braised Spicy Monkfish]

Agwi-jjim is prepared by braising monkfish with spices and vegetables. Monkfish meat is a delicacy with a rich and chewy texture, and develops a wonderful flavor when combined with Korean parsley and soy bean sprouts. Unlike other regions, dried monkfish is used to make this dish in Masan, the home of *agwi-jjim*.

Reborn as a Gourmet Dish

Monkfish used to be unpopular for its repulsive appearance—a gaping mouth fronting a flat head and body. When it was brought up in a net, the fishermen would simply toss it away or use it for fertilizer. Because the fish was hurled back into the water, they were known as *multeomengi*, or splashers. Thanks to the colorfully nicknamed "Lumpy Granny" who sold eel soup in Odong-dong, Masan, monkfish was reborn as a gourmet dish. She decided to braise monkfish the fishermen brought in—for some unknown reason—with garlic, scallion, soybean paste and hot pepper paste, in the style of *bugeo-jjim* (braised dried pollack). The dish and its interesting texture were unexpectedly well received. Monkfish was plentiful in the seas off the coast of Masan, so Lumpy Granny began including the dish on her menu as an accompaniment for drinks. Fifty years later, *agwi-jjim* has become a well-known delicacy throughout the nation.

Monkfish, a Low-fat and High-collagen Food

Monkfish tastes delicious despite its appearance. After it became popular, people began to wonder about its nutritional value and found out that the fish was rich in collagen, a group of proteins that enhances skin elasticity. For this reason, monkfish has become even more popular among women. Once considered an unlucky catch and discarded, monkfish has now become a local specialty of the Masan area, and there is even a "Monkfish Alley" in Odong-dong. Unlike other regions where fresh monkfish is used in *agwi-jjim*, the Masan *agwi-jjim* is made of dried monkfish. As if reflecting the character of South Gyeongsang people, *agwi-jjim* restaurants in Masan are sparsely decorated and the turnover is high. Everything is hurried, but at least no one has to wait a long time for a table.

Monkfish Liver, Another Foie Gras
In the *Agwi-jjim* Alley of Masan, *agwi-suyuk* (boiled monkfish) is also sold. This is basically boiled and sliced monkfish. Many claim that monkfish liver tastes better than the meat. Monkfish liver has become popular among gourmets, because of its similarity to foie gras.

The Ocean on a Platter
Haemul-jjim
[Braised Spicy Seafood]

Haemul-jjim is not much different from *agwi-jjim* in terms of spices and cooking process. The difference is the wide variety of seafood ingredients. *Haemul-jjim* features fresh blue crab, octopus, shrimp, mussels, clams, and sea squirt. It is truly a celebration of the full bounty of the sea.

Other Delicacies: Shrimp Head, Squid Roe, and Pollack Innards

Shrimp is a one of the main ingredients of *haemul-jjim*. When eating shrimp, many people savor the tail but discard the head. However, the head holds much of the unique flavor of the shrimp, as well as all sorts of nutrients. One is missing half the flavor if the shrimp head is thrown out. *Haemul-jjim* includes a variety of delicacies, such as crunchy sea squirt, squid roe, and pollack roe and testes. After fishing and eating the seafood in *haemul-jjim*, rice is mixed in the remaining sauce with chopped kimchi, Korean parsley, crushed dried laver, and sesame oil. Everything is mixed and stir-fried as a finishing course to the meal.

The Health Benefits of Seafood

Haemul-jjim fits the taste of contemporary people who prefer food that is delicious and healthy at the same time. Clams and other types of seafood are low in calories but high in protein, vitamins, and minerals. They boost the stamina and help to prevent lifestyle diseases. Lean, tender octopus, and flavorful squid are both rich in taurine, a substance known to alleviate fatigue. Furthermore, the chitosan in blue crab is known to bind fat and have a diuretic effect.

Making Fried Rice with Leftover Sauce
After eating the seafoods from *haemul-jjim*, one is left with a thick sauce. Chopped kimchi, Korean parsley and rice are mixed into the sauce and stir-fried all together to make a delicious rice dish. Sesame or perilla oil can be added for flavor.

A Salty and Spicy Side Dish
Galchi-jorim
[Braised Cutlassfish]

To make *galchi-jorim*, sweet autumn white radish or tender summer potatoes are placed in the bottom of a pot and topped with slabs of cutlassfish. A spicy sauce is then poured over the pot and the contents are braised. The dish consists of lean fish meat with radish or potatoes permeated with the spicy sauce.

Cutlassfish Braised in a Spicy Sauce

Until the 1980s, cutlassfish was considered a common fish that was served at the home. The thick body was salted and grilled or pan-fried, and the head and tail were braised in spicy sauce with white radish or potatoes. Unfortunately, the fish has since then become rare and expensive, hence the nickname "golden cutlassfish." A visitor to the Namdaemun Market in Seoul is greeted by the salty and spicy *galchi-jorim* drifting out of *Galchi-jorim* Alley. Typically cooked and served in well-worn and dented nickel silver pots, the red sweet-spicy sauce is excellent for mixing with rice, and the taste of soft radish drenched is to savor. The *galchi-jorim* alley is always bustling with hungry customers eagerly waiting in line. There are more than ten *galchi-jorim* restaurants in the alley that have been in business anywhere from 20 to 40 years.

How to Remove Bones from the Cutlassfish

How do skilled Korean diners remove the bones from cutlassfish? First, they poke holes along the edges of the fish and carefully pull out the pin bones in two neat rows. Some people become unbelievably good in executing this process. They set aside the small bone clusters from the edges. When separating the meat from the bone, the trick is to use the tip of a chopstick to carefully lift the upper meat little by little. Once enough space has been created between the meat and bone, a chopstick can be placed between them and run all the way to the tail to separate the top fillet. The same routine is followed for the other side. After eating the flesh, the small bone clusters removed in the first step can be nibbled on to get the tender meat from in between the bones.

Namdaemun Market *Galchi-jorim* in a Nickel Silver Pot

Fishy Smell Removed with a Spicy Sauce
Godeungeo-jorim
[Braised Mackerel]

Mackerel has always been an affordable and popular fish in Korea. It has been called "the barley of the sea," because it is as nourishing as barley. As a "blue-backed" oily fish, mackerel is rich with many nutrients including the brain-nourishing DHA.

Filled with Flesh and Flavor

There is an interesting term derived from the name of mackerel. In Japanese, mackerel is *saba*, and said twice becomes *saba-saba*. The colloquial Korean term *saba-saba* refers to flattery or under-the-table deals involving bribery. The word originated in the Japanese colonial era, when people asking a favor from a public official would offer two mackerels. This bribe repeatedly proved effective and, as a result, *saba-saba* became a term for flattery or bribery.

Perfect with Potatoes, White Radish and Aged Kimchi

The sauce for *godeungeo-jorim* is made by mixing a generous amount of red chili paste or red pepper flakes with soy sauce. Because mackerel can have a strong fishy smell, the sauce also includes generous dollops of garlic and ginger. The cooking process for *godeungeo-jorim* is almost identical to that of *galchi-jorim* (braised cutlassfish). Mackerel is braised on top of potatoes or white radish while the sauce is intermittently spooned over the fish. Mackerel goes especially well with potatoes. Recently a *godeungeo-jorim* variation that replaces the potatoes with aged kimchi and uses a sauce blended with *doenjang* (soybean paste) has become popular among restaurant goers.

Removing the fishy smell of mackerel is key to a tasty *godeungeo-jorim*. Ample garlic and ginger are added to achieve this. Sometimes, aged kimchi and soybean paste are added to enhance the flavor.

Autumn Mackerel
Autumn and winter mackerel taste the best. This is because, after June, when the spawning season ends, the fishs begin to prepare for winter by eating voraciously, accumulating fat and nutrients.

Expensive But Worth Every Penny
Eun-daegu-jorim
[Braised Black Cod]

Eun-daegu (black cod), although fatty, does not have an unpleasant smell nor does it contain the greasy taste of fatty tuna. It has a creamy texture, a luxurious flavor, and a clean after-taste. *Eun-daegu-jorim*, which is famous for its sweet and spicy taste, is a favorite seafood dish in Korea and can be found in most Korean food restaurants overseas.

A $50,000 Fish

Although a great amount of confusion surrounds it, *eun-daegu* is neither Chilean seabass nor cod. In English, it is called black cod, sablefish, butterfish, or coal fish. A limited number is caught off the coasts of Russia, British Colombia, Alaska, and other American states. This once-affordable fish used to be consumed mainly by Americans and British who salt-pickled and grilled it. However, as it became more and more popular around the globe, especially in Japan, the price has soared, and now it has become exorbitantly expensive. Since 1984, New South Wales, Australia has designated a similar fish, also called black cod, in the Southern Hemisphere as a vulnerable species and has banned harvest with a fine of over 50,000 dollars for illegal fishing. There are only twelve people in the world who have the license to fish this Arctic Ocean species in the wild.

A Firm yet Flaky Texture

Fatty *eun-daegu* is so tender that it flakes under the touch. Because the fish is mainly distributed frozen, it is often consumed fried, braised, or simmered. Koreans prefer it glazed with a sweet and spicy sauce, while Japanese gourmets, who prefer the mild and creamy taste, enjoy it raw or grilled. Americans and Canadians often enjoy the fish smoked. Thanks to the recent success of *eun-daegu* farming, more and more people are able to enjoy *eun-daegu* dishes including *hoe* (sliced raw fish).

Eun-daegu contains an abundance of calcium, phosphorus, iron, potassium, and vitamins. Packed with omega-3 fatty acids, it is effective against myocardial infarction and excellent for improving blood circulation.

Everyday Side Dish

Dubu-jorim

[Braised Tofu]

Dubu-jorim is simmered in a soy sauce mixture. *Dubu-jorim* is clean and tastes delicious even when cold, which made it a lunchbox staple in the past. With its delicate aroma of sesame oil, adding it to a simple meal of rice and kimchi would make anyone's mouth water. Indeed, it has long been an everyday side dish welcomed by all.

What is in Tofu?

The origins of the word "*kong*" (soybean) have yet to be established. However, one leading theory is that it was inspired by the sound of soybeans striking the floor. Soybeans are often called "beef from the field," because it is nutritionally similar to meat, although it is a legume. Protein makes up 40 percent of tofu, along with important nutrients including iron, calcium, magnesium, and vitamin B complex. The yellow color of most soybeans comes from isoflavones, a cancer-fighting substance that has become highly popular for its bioactive properties. The benefits of soybean and the nutritional value of tofu are well known in the West. It is rumored that tofu is now a leading ingredient in the US White House.

Easy-to-cook and Delicious Side Dishes

Dubu-jorim is tasty and easy to cook, even for those who lack confidence in the kitchen. Its flavor can vary with the marinade used, and the only trick lies in removing the water carefully to prevent the oil from spattering.

If dusted with starch before frying, it can be made even crispier and more savory.

A Popular Drinking Accompaniment
Dubu-kimchi
[Tofu with Stir-fried Kimchi]

Tofu and kimchi together make an ideal combination. *Dubu-kimchi* refers to warm sliced tofu served with boiled or sautéed kimchi. Mild-tasting tofu rich in protein is a perfect complement to spicy kimchi and its abundant vitamins. Many Koreans like to eat *dubu-kimchi* while enjoying *soju* (a Korean distilled spirit) or *makgeolli* (Korean rice wine).

Tofu as a Celebrity Diet Food

It is well known that so-called one-food diets are detrimental to health. But many Korean celebrities who successfully lost weight say that tofu is an exception to this rule. Tofu is an essential part of the diet for many celebrities who want to maintain a super slim figure. Shindong, a member of the boy band Super Junior, lost 44 pounds in four and half months with a *dubu-kimchi* diet. Sol Kyung-gu, who is known for repeatedly gaining or losing weight for movie roles, says that he literally lived on tofu when he had to lose 30 pounds in a single month. Recounting how he fought hunger with only tofu and cucumbers, the actor says: "Tofu is unbeatable if you want to lose weight fast."

A Great Harmony of Red and White

Dubu-kimchi is a dish that anyone can easily make with some kimchi and a block of bean curd from the refrigerator. Just find an attractive serving dish, and the most ordinary cooking ingredients can become a colorful gourmet dish.

The amino acid lysine found in soybeans—the main component of bean curd—is an essential nutrient for growing children. In addition, as a high-protein and low-calorie food, bean curd is ideal for those who want to stay fit and energized at the same time.

Korea's Favorite Snack
Tteok-bokki
[Stir-fried Rice Cake]

Tteok-bokki is representative of hot Korean dishes spiced with red chili paste. Everybody loves *tteok-bokki*. Even children, who have yet to develop a taste for spicy food, enjoy *tteok-bokki*, even if they have to drink lots of water to cool their tongue. It is the national street food of Korea.

Gungjung tteok-bokki, A Colorful Dish for Royalties

Originally, *tteok-bokki* was not a spicy dish. In the royal courts (*gungjung*) of Joseon, it was prepared by simmering beef, carrots, onions, shiitake, and other ingredients together with rice cakes in soy sauce. The colorful ingredients—black shiitake, white onions, red carrots and peppers, green chili peppers, and yellow egg garnish—were visually as well as nutritionally harmonious.

Gochujang tteok-bokki Debuts in the 1950s

It is believed that *tteok-bokki* seasoned with spicy red chili paste (*gochujang*) first appeared in the 1950s and became widely popular in the 1970s. Because *tteok-bokki* in this early incarnation was a working-class snack, flour, instead of rice, was used to make the finger-like *tteok* sticks. The dish was an instant hit and became the most popular snack item along with fish cake (*eomuk*) soup. The history of the Sindang-dong *Tteok-bokki* Alley, which is the most famous row of *tteok-bokki* shops in Korea, dates back to the 1970s. There was once a famous *tteok-bokki* restaurant named "Babodeul" (Fools). To please its student clientele, the restaurant installed a music system and hired an amateur DJ to play songs on request. Their romantic concept of "listening to favorite songs while enjoying *tteok-bokki*" proved extremely popular and led to the establishment of numerous restaurants under similar themes.

Gungjung tteok-bokki for Healthy Skin
Gungjung tteok-bokki, which combines meat with vegetables, is a nutritionally balanced dish. The vitamins in carrots and cabbage promote red blood cell production and healthy skin. The gooey substance in the straw mushrooms gives luster to the skin, and the fibers help the body flush out toxins.

A Dish that Will Bring Tears to Your Eyes
Nakji-bokkeum
[Stir-fried Octopus]

Nakji-bokkeum is made with common octopus, onions, scallion, red and green chili peppers, anchovy or littleneck clam broth, and a spicy sauce. The sauce is made by blending red pepper flakes and minced garlic with sugar, soy sauce and red pepper paste. Mugyo-dong and Jongno are the place to go for extra spicy *nakji-bokkeum* packed with garlic and *cheongyang* peppers.

The Legendary Story of Mugyo-dong *Nakji* Alley

Mugyo-dong *Nakji,* a variation of *nakji-bokkeum,* was created by Bak Mu-sun, the living legend of Mugyo-dong *Nakji* Alley. Back when *nakji* (baby or common octopus) was cheap and plentiful, Bak opened a working class eatery in the center of Seoul and served *nakji-bokkeum,* clear clam soup, *gamja-tang* (pork backbone soup), and *pajeon* (green onion pancake). Although it was just a simple dish meant to accompany a kettle of *makgeolli* (Korean rice wine), her ferociously spicy *nakji-bokkeum* captured the fancy of every drinker in town. Restaurants mimicking her recipe began to sprout up all along the alley. Yujeong and Mijeong are the most famous among them. Bak's legacy continues even today under the household name "Mugyo-dong *Nakji*."

As a low-calorie/high-protein food, octopus is good for a diet or just when in need of refreshment. It is rich in minerals such as calcium and phosphorus, and contains a rich supply of taurine which is highly effective in building muscle and protecting cardiovascular health.

Spicy and Sweet Flavor
Ojingeo-bokkeum
[Stir-fried Squid]

To make *ojingeo-bokkeum*, stir-fry parboiled squid in sauce over high heat. The sauce is created by blending garlic and onions with *gochujang*. It is sweet and zesty, yet spicy enough to make even the most seasoned Korean diners sweat. *Ojingeo-bokkeum* is one of the most popular dishes using the firm-textured and flavorful squid.

Squid, a Versatile Seafood

With squid, there is nothing to throw out. There are many recipes that use the head, legs, and even the innards. For example, squid entrails are the main ingredient of *ojingeo-naejangtang* (squid innards soup). People in Ulleungdo, an island famous for squid fishing, claim that the best way to enjoy the full flavor of squid is to slice and eat steamed whole squid, innards, and all. Grilled dried squid is a popular movie snack or a late night snack for students. Nowadays there are many variations of *ojingeo-bulgogi* (marinated and grilled squid), including recipes that add pork belly or herbal roots.

Squid goes well with a variety of vegetables since, as an acid-residue food, it contains more phosphorus than calcium. Tossing in some vegetables, which are alkaline, means adding vitamins A and C. In particular, squid and cabbage cooked together become a diet food that even helps regularity.

Energy for a Tired Body
Jeyuk-bokkeum
[Stir-fried Pork]

Jeyuk-bokkeum is one of the best-known dishes cooked with *gochujang*. It is a stir-fried dish with thick slices of a pork shoulder marinated in *gochujang* with minced ginger. Before the 1950s, it was reportedly made using only scallion, black pepper, and soy sauce, and the current form of *jeyuk-bokkeum* marinated in *gochujang* is believed to have appeared sometime afterwards.

An Affordable Dish Served in Generous Portions

Koreans associate beef with *bulgogi* and pork with *jeyuk-bokkeum*. *Jeyuk-bokkeum* appears on the menu of virtually every Korean restaurant in the world and has won the hearts of diners of all nationalities. *Gochujang* eliminates any unpleasant smell of pork and tenderizes the fatty meat. Because pork fat contains a high percentage of highly unsaturated fatty acids such as oleic acid and linoleic acid, pork tastes best when cooked over moderate heat. Pork has eight to ten times more vitamin B1 than beef, and its digestion rate can be as high as 95 percent. Young people on limited budgets favor *jeyuk-bokkeum*, because it is a hearty meat dish yet inexpensive. Youngsters often list it as their favorite food, and many Korean mothers will talk about how their son can "finish a pound of *jeyuk-bokkeum* on a sitting."

How to Obtain a Lustrous Glaze

Preheat the pan before sautéing the marinated pork. To prevent the dish from getting soupy, keep the lid off the pan to let the liquids in the meat and vegetables evaporate. It is important to control the heat, because too much will burn the sauce yet leave the inside of the meat uncooked. Set aside some of the sauce and later add to the pan. Toss immediately before serving, in order to coat the meat and create a glazed appearance. Add perilla leaves for a zesty flavor and fragrance. Half-split garlic cloves are another great addition. Garlic is rich in allicin, which has powerful anti-bacterial and anti-coagulant effects.

Pork helps prevent cholesterol from sticking to the walls of arteries, strengthening blood vessels, and combating a number of lifestyle diseases. In addition, its vitamin B1 content is ten times greater than that of beef.

GUI & JEON
[Grilled Dishes and Pan-fried Delicacies]

Unlike Western cuisine where grilling is largely limited to steak or barbecued foods, grilling in Korean cuisine is a more common cooking method applied to a great variety of ingredients. It is also open to a broad range of flavors, depending on whether marinades are applied, and if so, the type of marinade sauce. *Galbi-gui* (grilled short ribs) is popular among Koreans and foreigners alike. *Jeon* (pan-fried dishes), made with a cooking process which requires only a small amount of oil, is a healthy dish loved by all.

Marinated, Chargrilled Short Ribs
So-galbi-gui
[Grilled Beef Ribs]

So-galbi-gui refers to marinated beef short ribs grilled over a charcoal stove on the table. Tender ribs of young cattle are considered best for *so-galbi-gui*. In the past, the ribs used to be marinated in a light colored and saltier soy sauce known as *joseon ganjang*. Nowadays, the darker regular soy sauce is used with some salt. The marinating process is skipped altogether for *saenggalbi-gui* (un-marinated grilled beef ribs).

Suwon-galbi, Famous for Generous Servings

So-galbi-gui is cooked on a grill, which is placed over fine-textured oak charcoal at a red-hot temperature. Its biggest appeal is the smoky flavor from the charcoal. It is crucial to skillfully score the ribs in order to allow the meat to be thoroughly marinated and grilled without burning. Great care is required as it is not easy to butterfly and score the meat and still keep it attached to the bone.

Suwon in Gyeonggi Province is especially famous for *so-galbi-gui*. It is said that Hwachu-nok, which opened in the Yeongdong Market in Paldal-gu in the 1940s, was known as the first *so-galbi-gui* restaurant in the region. It is not in business anymore, but the secret to its unique flavor remains, characterized by its method of using salt and sweet pear juice instead of soy sauce. *Suwon-galbi*, sectioned with an axe, is very large, and the meat attached on both sides of the ribs provides for generous servings.

Haeundae-galbi and *Idong-galbi*

Haeundae, Busan is also a famous *galbi* town. Marinated *haeundae-galbi* is not cooked on a grill but on a steel plate. The beef juice left on the plate is delicious when mixed with rice. Pocheon, Gyeonggi Province, was once home to many military bases. Targeting mothers who wanted to feed their sons while on military leave, a number of *galbi* restaurants sprouted up in the area. These restaurants are known as *idong-galbi*, and are famous for their moderate price and generous portions.

The Menu of Choice on Special Days

Even today, the expensive *so-galbi-gui* is reserved for special occasions. In fact, it was only in the 1980s, when the nation became relatively affluent, that average Koreans could afford to dine out at *galbi* restaurants. At the time, many *galbi* restaurants opened in the outskirts of big cities, invariably including the word "garden" or "park" in their name. People donned their best clothes and celebrated special occasions at *galbi* "gardens" and "parks," and were seen leaving with toothpicks dangling from their mouths. The conspicuous use of toothpicks was a way to show off and let everyone know that they had dined on *galbi*.

Reassembled and Grilled Short Ribs
Tteok-galbi
[Grilled Short Rib Patties]

Tteok-galbi was a royal beef dish once enjoyed by kings. Its name comes from its similarity in appearance to steamed rice cakes. One story has it that as palatable as *so-galbi-gui* is, it was not befitting for kings to bite off the meat from the ribs and, hence, *tteok-galbi* was born. It is a dish that is easier to eat, although not necessarily easier on the chef.

Royal Cuisine Learned from Court Ladies and Exiled Nobilities

Koreans love their *galbi*. However, it is not easy for children or the elderly with weak teeth to pull the meat off the bones. In this case, *tteok-galbi* is a perfect alternative. Originally a royal dish, *tteok-galbi* is now a famous local specialty of Gwangju and Yangju, Gyeonggi Province and Damyang and Hwasun, South Jeolla Province. The recipes of Gyeonggi Province *tteok-galbi* are said to have been imparted from court ladies in the late Joseon era. Minced rib meat is seasoned and wrapped around the bone to create a shape resembling steamed rice cakes. This is char-grilled to produce a wonderfully chewy texture.

The recipe for South Jeolla *tteok-galbi* was reportedly passed on by nobilities in exile. The most famous of these is Damyang *tteok-galbi*, which was passed on by Song Hui-gyeong around 650 years ago. *Tteok-galbi*, which exclusively uses rib meat, is best when infused with the aroma of charred oak.

A Combination of Prime *Galbi* Meat, Marinade, and Smoky Fragrance

Near Songjeong in Gwangju, South Jeolla Province there is a *tteok-galbi* street specializing in *tteok-galbi* made with half beef and half pork. Its history dates back to the 1950s, when Choe Cheo-ja began to sell *tteok-galbi* with *bibimbap*. Back then in the Songjeong market, there was a slaughterhouse and a cattle market, which provided her with easy access to meat and the opportunity to create inexpensive, savory *tteok-galbi*. Her recipe requires that the meat be hand-kneaded for a long time in the seasoning made from nearly 20 ingredients including kelp, pear, and honey to ensure thorough marination. Also, a special sauce is intermittently brushed on the meat while it is slowly grilled over charcoal.

---

* Song Hui-gyeong was sent to Japan in 1420 as an emissary of King Sejong during the early Joseon period. There, he was pressured to sign using the Japanese reign title instead of that of the Ming dynasty. He refused to give into this demand, and won the admiration of the Japanese king.

A Sumptuous, Affordable Dish for the Masses

Dwaeji-galbi-gui

[Grilled Spareribs]

Dwaeji-galbi-gui is more affordable than the expensive *so-galbi-gui*, and its soft texture makes it easy to chew and digest. Pork ribs are marinated in a mixture made with plenty of minced ginger and black pepper to remove any porky smell. Because of the captivating image of sizzling *dwaeji-galbi-gui* on the grill, this dish is often featured in foreign newspapers.

A Barrel of Flavor

Among the numerous *dwaeji-galbi-gui* restaurants, the most famous are the ones in the Mapo *Dwaeji-galbi-gui* Street in Seoul. Prior to the 1950s, the Mapo marina bustled with cargo boats, and timber and grains that had traveled down the Han River in the boats passed through Mapo to reach central Seoul. For this reason, there were many sawmills and granaries around the dock. In the evenings, workers used to look for something to "scrub" sawdust from their throat, and cheap eateries selling pork and *makgeolli* (Korean rice wine) opened up in the region to meet their needs. However, with the construction of railroads, the dock was closed down, and the blue-collar workers were gradually replaced with white-collar workers and local merchants, looking to enjoy some *soju* (Korean distilled spirit) with snacks on their way home from work. Unlike today's restaurants that have individual ventilators for each table, *dwaeji-galbi-gui* diners in the past were filled with so much smoke that one could hardly see. Meat was grilled on a table made out of junk oil barrels, containing briquette stoves inside. These oil-drum tables would be surrounded with three or four stools barely large enough to sit on. But the food and drinks were merry, and all doors and windows were kept open to disperse the smoke.

A Nutritious Treat When Served with Lettuce, Perilla Leaves, and Raw Garlic

Regardless of the times, *dwaeji-galbi-gui* is always served and eaten the same way. The meat is wrapped in lettuce or perilla leaves along with raw garlic and chili pepper, and dipped in *ssamjang* (a spicy, pungent mixed sauce). Sometimes, a small fire-resistant bowl containing sesame oil is placed on the grill to cook garlic. Seasoning determines the taste of *dwaeji-galbi-gui*, because the dish uses the first five ribs of a pig, which tends to have an unpleasant porky smell. Seasoned with a soy sauce marinade, *dwaeji-galbi-gui* is usually eaten with raw vegetables to achieve nutritional balance.

Koreans' Favorite Meat Dish
Bulgogi
[*Bulgogi*]

Bulgogi is prepared by marinating thin slices of beef and grilling them. In the past, the royal court and *yangbans* (gentry class) in Seoul used to call it *neobiani*, which means wide meat slices.

The Origin of *Bulgogi*: *Maekjeok* in Goguryeo

Traditional grilled meat dishes in Korea originated from *maekjeok*. *Maek* was the northeast region of China, and is also a reference to Goguryeo which is one of the earliest Korean kingdoms. *Maekjeok* is a dish of barbecued beef skewers and, according to folklore, it evolved into the current *bulgogi* because the introduction of the grill made skewers obsolete. It is said that *bulgogi* was the only dish in the world that marinated the meat before it is grilled. There is a similar dish in China, but the meat is grilled or ground first and then mixed with sauce. Because the marinated *maekjeok* did not require the use of sauce, it was also called *mujang* (no sauce). It eventually evolved into a royal court dish *neobiani*, the predecessor of *bulgogi*.

Mixing Rice with the Juicy Broth

Bulgogi tastes sweet and flavorful because it is marinated in a sauce consisting of honey, thick soy sauce, black pepper, chopped garlic, and scallion. Back when restaurants did not offer as many choices as now, Koreans usually ate *bulgogi* when they dined out on special days. While the *bulgogi* sizzled on a plate moist with its juice, adults ate the meat and drank *suju* (Korean distilled spirit), and children mixed their rice with the sweet gravy.

President Obama and *Bulgogi*
Bulgogi has long been a popular dish served to guests. Many foreigners visiting Korea are impressed by *bulgogi*, and state guests are no exception. Indeed, US President Barack Obama, a known fan of Korean cuisine, cites *bulgogi* as one of his favorite lunch choices. During his 2009 state visit to Korea, Cheongwadae (presidential residence) gladly obliged and served *bulgogi* at the official dinner.

The Gravy Which Is Tastier than the Meat
Ttukbaegi-bulgogi
[Hot Pot *Bulgogi*]

Ttukbaegi-bulgogi is made by adding water and cooking *bulgogi* in a clay pot. The meat becomes tender and releases succulent juices into the water, resulting in a gravy which is great for mixing with rice. This dish is a good alternative for single diners who crave *bulgogi* but lack the company.

Ttukbaegi Straight onto the Table

Ttukbaegi (clay pot) is a convenient cooking vessel. It does not break even when placed over a direct flame and can be set on the table even when it is hot. Once heated, the pot retains heat and keeps the food warm for the duration of the meal. Many dishes are served in a clay pot, including *seolleong-tang* (ox bone soup), *galbi-tang* (short rib soup), *doenjang-jjigae* (soybean paste stew), *kimchi-jjigae* (kimchi stew), and *yukgaejang* (spicy beef soup). However, *ttukbaegi-bulgogi* is the only dish that has "clay pot" in its name.

Ideal for Individual Dining

Up until about two to three decades ago, *bulgogi* was consumed like a hotpot dish. Back then, the *bulgogi* grill was in a concave shape unlike the convex ones used these days. Vegetables were placed in the hollowed middle and marinated meat placed alongside the higher rim. The meat broth flowed down into the center and cooked the vegetables. The resulting gravy, rich with the flavor of *bulgogi*, was delicious when mixed with rice. With the passage of time, however, people began to prefer the meat over the rice-gravy mix. Restaurants complied with the demand, and introduced convex grills to cook *bulgogi*. But people started to miss the combination of *bulgogi* gravy and rice, and so the idea of cooking *bulgogi* in a clay pot emerged. *Ttukbaegi-bulgogi* is popular, especially among lone diners as well as children and elders who like the soft texture of rice mixed moistened with gravy.

The *ttukbaegi*, a traditional Korean clay pot, is still in wide use even today. Varying in size and shape, they are perfect for holding hot foods like *jjigae* (stew) in the wintertime, since they are slow to cool once heated.

Vegetables Wrapped in Seared Beef
Sogogi-pyeonchae
[Sliced Beef with Vegetables]

Sogogi-pyeonchae is a cold summer dish made by freezing smoked strip loin, slightly thawing it, and sliced into thin pieces. The lean strip loin combined with various vegetables makes this fresh-tasting dish a classic.

An Appetizer Favored by Foreigners

Surprisingly, many foreigners who have tried *sogogi-pyeonchae* say that it is the most memorable among the dishes they had in Korea. They say it's because the dish does not feel foreign, and does not taste strange or disagreeable. Although it is seared, it is close to *yuk-hoe* (beef tartare). However, because vegetables are wrapped in the beef slices and it is dipped in a spicy mustard soy sauce, it is easier to eat than regular uncooked meat. Its popularity can also be attributed to the fact that cold dishes are somewhat easier for foreigners to consume than the many boiling hot dishes, and that it goes well with red wine. It is elegantly presented with a small mound of vegetables in the middle, and thin meat slices placed around it.

Hot *Sogogi-pyeonchae*

Sogogi-pyeonchae can also be eaten hot, cooked at the table. The beef is seasoned with salt and black pepper, coated with sweet rice powder and pan-fried. A variety of sliced vegetables are placed on the meat slice, rolled up, and dipped in sauce. Surprisingly, even tougher cuts of meat become tender when coated with sweet rice powder and cooked. Sweet rice powder takes the greasy edge off the meat while preserving its flavor and nutrients.

Perilla Leaves, a Fragrant Accompaniment

Among the many vegetables that accompany *sogogi-pyeonchae*, perilla leaves (*kkaennip*) are the most appetizing. The leaves, commonly consumed by Koreans, are rich in antocyanin, a potent antioxidant. Perilla leaf extract is known to be highly effective in suppressing inflammation, allergic reactions, fat cell division and genes that accumulate fat cells. For such effects, it is often used to treat obesity.

Koreans' National Pork Dish

Samgyeopsal-gui

[Grilled Pork Belly]

Samgyeopsal, meaning "three layered meat," is the Korean name for pork belly. The pork belly is Koreans' favorite cut of pork. Some even say that Koreans consume all the pork belly in the world. Naturally, pork belly is the priciest pork cut in Korea.

Koreans' Insatiable Appetite for Pork Belly

The pork belly consumption in Korea exceeds imagination. According to statistics, the average Korean eats a serving of *samgyeopsal-gui* once every four days. Koreans take their pork belly seriously: there is a Samsam Day (March 3rd), designated for eating pork belly, and there is a spike in pork belly sales during the spring yellow dust season owing to the popular belief that pork belly will melt away the dust accumulated in the throat. The disproportional popularity of pork belly results in sluggish sales of other pork parts, and triggers campaigns promoting pork fillet, loin, shank, shoulder, and hock. *Mok-samgyeop* (three-layered pork neck) and *ogyeopsal* (five layered pork) are recently coined terms reflecting the popularity of pork belly. *Mok-samgyeop* was made to promote the cheaper neck/shoulder cut by associating it with *samgyeopsal*, whereas *ogyeopsal* is actually *samgyeopsal* with the skin attached.

When Did Koreans Begin to Eat Pork Belly?

Once the most unpopular and fatty cut of pork, pork belly was transformed into the tastiest cut by Gaeseong merchants who are traditionally known for their commercial flair. Raising western pig breeds, they discovered how to obtain the ideal pork belly. Pigs are omnivorous and can be fed on leftover food. People in Jeju Island even raised them in outhouses, raising them on human waste. As Gaeseong merchants alternated fiber-rich millet with condensed feed, they found the combination to produce the perfect pork belly with streaky layers of fat and meat. The savory blend of fat and meat captured the palate of Koreans, sending the price and popularity of *samgyeopsal* soaring.

Samgyeopsal-gui and Changing Trends

The early 1990s saw the rising popularity of pork belly slices grilled on iron pot lids. Shortly after, there was the *daepae samgyeopsal-gui* (shaved pork belly), which made it even cheaper than most restaurant meals. In the late 1990s, *misutgaru samgyeopsal-gui* (pork belly with a three grain powder) was the rage, and since 2000, it became fashionable to marinate pork belly in red wine or sprinkle it with green tea powder to reduce the greasy taste.

The Perennial Side Dish
Saengseon-gui
[Grilled Fish]

A piece of *saengseon-gui* somehow completes the Korean meal. Consequently, people have devised various ways to grill fish. Among them, sprinkling coarse sea salt and grilling, or intermittently brushing the fish with a soy sauce mix during grilling are the two most common ways of grilling a fish. Sometimes, red pepper paste is used for less salty fish. *Gulbi-gui* (grilled dried yellow croaker) and *godeungeo-gui* (grilled mackerel) are the most popular grilled fish dishes.

Gulbi-gui and Rice, a Perfect Summer Meal

Gulbi (dried yellow croaker) is made by salting and drying yellow croaker. It is non-greasy and has a slight sweet taste. The most delicious and thus expensive *gulbi* comes from Beopsseong-po off the coast of Yeonggwang, South Jeolla Province. In the past, people called dried yellow croaker *gubi-jogi* (bent yellow croaker) because the dried fish would bend in shape when it was strung in dried rice straw ropes and hung to dry. The word *gubi-jogi* evolved into *gulbi* as time passed. *Gulbi* fans say the summer is the best season to eat *gulbi*. Well-dried *gulbi* flesh is torn into strips and dipped in red pepper paste mixed with sesame oil. This is eaten with cooked rice immersed in icy cold water: nothing else is needed.

Gan-godeungeo-gui, Originated in the Remote Valley of Andong

Because Andong, North Gyeongsang Province is landlocked in the past, mackerel had to be transported all the way from the Ganggu Port in Yeongdeok. It took at least two days to deliver the fish through narrow mountain roads. Before the introduction of freezers, mackerel merchants salted mackerel to keep it from spoiling. Surprisingly, the salted mackerel proved to be much better than raw fish when grilled, thanks to the combination of the salt and the enzymes produced right before decomposition. As a result, Andong *gan-godeungeo* (salted mackerel) was born. The dish became so famous that everyone visiting Andong tried it, and through word of mouth Andong *gan-godeungeo* became famous, resulting in the emergence of commercial mackerel products labeled "Andong *gan-godeungeo*."

There is a wide variety of seasonal fish caught on the Korea peninsula. The favorites have been yellow croaker (*jogi*) in spring, salted mackerel (*gan-go deungeo*) in summer, cutlassfish (*galchi*) in fall and herring (*cheongeo*) in winter.

Weathered in the Wind and Sun
Hwangtae-gui
[Grilled Dried Pollack]

Hwangtae-gui refers to seasoned grilled dried pollack. Whole well-dried pollack is split and butterflied, cut into pieces, and grilled while brushing liberally with a red pepper paste sauce mixture. *Hwangtae-gui*, an ideal winter delicacy, is popular as an accompaniment to *soju* (a Korean distilled spirit) but also as salty side dish to be eaten with rice.

Myeongtae: Nothing Goes to Waste

For Koreans, pollack (*myeongtae*) is more than just a fish. It has traditionally been closely associated with for good fortune. The remnants of this custom can still be seen today when dried pollacks are tied in string and hung in a newly moved-in house or a newly open business. Dried pollack is one of the key foods offered in sacrificial rites and ancestral rites performed on holidays. There is no other fish that is consumed as thoroughly as dried pollack: the eyes are stir-fried and served as a side dish with drinks; the steamed skin is consumed as wraps; the innards are salted and fermented to become a side dish called *changnan-jeot*; salted and fermented gills are known as *agami-jeot*; and salted and fermented roe becomes *myeongnan-jeot*.

Hwangtae: Repeatedly Frozen and Thawed in the Wind

Hwangtae refers to a certain variety of dried pollack. However, it is different from the regular dried pollack (*bugeo*) in that it undergoes a curing process that requires extreme care. It is repeatedly frozen and thawed in mountainous areas where temperatures fall below -10°C. *Hwangtae* is made by hanging whole pollacks for 40 to 90 days in a windy, freezing outdoor environment. Over the course of weeks, the pollack slowly dries, freezes at night and thaws during the day. After repeated contractions and expansions, the fish finally turns into a yellowish *hwangtae*. Although it is still a form of dried fish, *hwangtae* appears plump as if rehydrated in water. The flesh is white, soft and has a savory taste free from any fishy smell. The key to producing the tastiest possible *hwangtae* is the weather. If it continues to be severely cold, *hwangtae* reaches its peak. In contrast, if the weather warms up early, that year's *hwangtae* turns out as *meoktae*, a term that describes a darker and less ideal *hwangtae*.

The Best Cure for Hangovers

Hwangtae has long been recognized for cleansing the body of toxins, and protecting the liver. It has been widely used in soup specially prepared to cure hangovers. In fact, many people say they feel much better after a night of heavy drinking when they consume *hwangtae*.

The easiest way to eat *hwangtae* is to brew it into a stock. Once the stock has been prepared by simmering *hwangtae*, you can drink it at leisure or use it in cooking.

A Nutritious Dish for Tight Budgets
Chuncheon-dak-galbi
[Chuncheon Style Spicy Stir-fried Chicken]

Chuncheon-dak-galbi is a dish prepared by pan-frying chicken that has been marinated in a mixture of *gochujang* and vegetables in a large round iron skillet. Known together with *mak-guksu* (buckwheat noodles with vegetables) as a representative local dish of Chuncheon, it is now enjoyed nationwide, particularly among college students on limited budgets.

A Splendid Makeover of *Gyereuk**

Dak-galbi restaurants in Inje and Wontong, Gangwon Province are among the local attractions enjoyed by people visiting loved ones stationed at the military bases that populate the area. *Chuncheon-dak-galbi* first gained fame as an inexpensive dish favored by students. Although several opinions remain as to who exactly first created *dak-galbi*, the general consensus is that it was Kim Yeong-seok, a restauranteur once specializing in pork in the Jungangno area of Chuncheon in the 1960s. Even the local government of Chuncheon has validated the story as part of the city's official history in order to establish the city as the origin of *dak-galbi*. One day in the early 1960s, Mr. and Mrs. Kim, who were then selling pork dishes in their restaurant, ran out of pork. They rushed to a nearby store, bought two chickens and cooked them in the same way they would cook pork ribs. They split and spread out the chicken meat like pork ribs, grilled and sliced it, and discovered it has a unique savory flavor. They later introduced grilled chicken marinated in a sugary sauce and it became a big hit.

Dak-galbi: Value for Money

The owners of *dak-galbi* restaurants proudly claim that the portions, price, and taste of *dak-galbi* are unrivaled. Today, *dak-galbi* is reputed as a great dish that combines chicken with an assortment of healthy vegetables. It has grown popular among international diners as well. The recipe for *chuncheon dak-galbi* is as follows: Cut up and marinate a medium-sized chicken in a *gochujang* sauce for seven to eight hours. Cut cabbage, sweet potato, carrot, perilla leaves, and other vegetables and greens into bite-size pieces. Heat a well-oiled pan and stir-fry the chicken pieces together with the vegetables. Everyone has their favorite ingredient: some will eat the rice cake sticks first, while others go for sweet potatoes. Thus, almost every *dak-galbi* restaurant offers extra ingredients that can be added to the pan according to different tastes. Once most of the pan is empty, rice is stir-fried in the remaining sauce for a finishing touch.

Chicken is good for the skin and can be helpful to patients with osteoporosis. Rich in protein, it stimulates brain activity as its abundant essential amino acids increase the levels of excitatory neurotransmitters and help relieve stress.

*Gyereuk
When Cao Cao of China first said the word "*gyereuk*," his subordinates could not figure out what he meant. The word means "chicken ribs" which is not as fleshy as the leg or breast, yet a shame to just throw away. In this sense, the word "*gyereuk*" is used as a metaphor for something that you hesitate to abandon even though it is of little use to you.

A Hearty Dish for True Gourmets
Gopchang-gui
[Grilled Beef Tripe]

Gopchang is divided into *so-gopchang* and *yang-gopchang*. *So-gopchang* indicates the small intestine of a cow while *yang-gopchang* refers to its first stomach. A cow has four stomachs: The first is called the rumen (*yang*); the second the reticulum (*cheonyeop*); the third the omasum (*jeolchang*); and the fourth the abomasums (*makchang*).

Beef Innards as a Superb Ingredient

The taste of *gopchang-gui* hinges on eliminating any unpleasant odors. Marinating beef chitterlings in onion juice in the refrigerator for two to three hours helps tenderize the meat and purge odors. In the past, *gopchang* was usually eaten by commoners who could not afford more expensive meat. Accordingly, *gopchang* houses were mainly humble affairs equipped with large oil drums made into tables and a couple of shabby chairs. However, things have changed dramatically. As *gopchang* became a delicacy and more expensive than regular meat, today's *gopchang* restaurants have become high-end and now sport stylish interiors. When cooked to perfection, the outside of the chitterling is crispy and golden brown, while the inside remains soft and juicy. With a savory taste and pleasant texture, *gopchang-gui* is welcomed by drinkers as the best accompaniment to *soju* (Korean distilled spirit).

A Perfect Accompaniment for Drinking

Gopchang is perfect to invigorate weakened constitutions and to speed postpartum recovery. As a high-protein, low-calorie food, it protects the lining of the stomach and helps break down alcohol. In this sense, *gopchang* is a welcome dish for business entertainment or at office parties.

Gopchang is a high-protein food. As long as cholesterol intake is kept in check, it can be considered a health food richer in iron and vitamins than other forms of meat. It reinvigorates weakened constitutions and is perfect for patients recovering from illness.

A Food for Both Health and Beauty
Ori-gui
[Grilled Duck]

Duck is well-known for cleansing the body and ridding it of toxins. It is also a restorative food for patients coming off surgery or recovering from illness. These days, duck has also become popular as a beauty food, since its high collagen content was discovered to be beneficial for the skin.

A Boon of a Meal

In the past, duck was given the cold shoulder. The meat was unpopular, because it lacked the lean and savory quality of chicken and gave off an unpleasant gamy smell. There are even old phrases that reflect the negative perceptions toward duck, such as "to hold out a duck's foot after eating a chicken," which refers to a guilty person brazenly claiming innocence. Another phrase "duck eggs in the Nakdong River," means someone feeling unwanted and useless. However, duck has suddenly become popular recently due to new evidence showing that duck helps to detoxify the body and strengthen the immune system and build resistance. According to studies, ducks fed on sulfur, which can be toxic in nature, ends up having medicinal effects. Duck meat contains up to 45 percent unsaturated fatty acids, a substantially higher number compared to other meats. Unsaturated fatty acids do not build up in the vessels, and therefore one can eat as much duck as one wants without worrying about the health consequences. With proper cooking, duck meat becomes tender, flavorful, and low in fat content. Now, *ori-gui* is considered a more luxurious dish than *tongdak-gui* (roast whole chicken).

Grilled Cuisine with a Unique Flavor

Grilling is the most fundamental form of cooking and usually involves applying dry heat of 200-300 degrees Celsius to food. Grilled at high temperatures, duck meat acquires a flavor different than when it is boiled in water. At high temperatures, dehydration occurs on the surface of the meat, leading to the concentration of flavorful compounds. In addition, during the process of grilling, a smoky aroma similar to that of a charcoal fire is added, providing a distinctive flavor.

The Mountain Meat
Deodeok-gui
[Grilled Bonnet Bellflower Root]

The aroma of wild *deodeok* (bonnet bellflower root) can be sensed even from a great distance. Sweet and pleasantly bitter, it is claimed that wild *deodeok* grows on dewdrops in the mountainsides. *Deodeok* is rich in fiber and has earned the nickname "mountain meat" because of its firm, chewy texture. In China, *deodeok* has been used purely as a medicinal herb, but Koreans have used it mostly for cooking.

Evidence that Food Is Medicine

Since ancient times, wild *deodeok* has been referred to as *"sasam* (ginseng grown on sand),*"* because of the belief that its pharmacological effects are comparable to wild ginseng. According to old sayings, *deodeok* can relieve even the nastiest stomach cramps. *Deodeok* is similar to ginseng or wild bellflower in appearance but has a distinct flavor. It is preferred over bellflower roots, because the root is more fragrant and tender. Young leaves of *deodeok* can be steamed and eaten as a side dish or as wraps, while the roots are used in various dishes including *gochujang-jangajji* (*deodeok* roots pickled in red hot pepper paste), *saengchae* (julienned *deodeok* root salad), *jaban* (salted *deodeok* roots), *gui* (grilled *deodeok* roots), *nureumjeok* (pan-fried *deodeok* roots), *jeonggwa* (candied *deodeok* roots), and *deodeok* root liquor. Among these, it is *deodeok-gui* that makes the best side dish for rice. *Deodeok-gui*, prepared by brushing the roots with a *gochujang* sauce and grilling it in an oiled pan or over charcoal flames, has a deliciously tender and crunchy texture.

How to Peel Wild *Deodeok*
After cleansing the surface of the wild *deodeok* with a scouring pad, soak it in boiling water for four or five seconds. Because the sticky saponins smear into the *deodeok*, it becomes easier to peel with a knife or other tool. Do not rinse the peeled *deodeok*, just lightly pound it with the back of a knife or dowel until tender and then prepare it to taste grilled or pickled in red chili paste.

The Rainy Day Griddlecake
Pajeon
[Green Onion Pancake]

Pajeon is a mixture of wheat flour batter and scallions shallow-fried on a griddle. It goes wonderfully well with chilled *dongdongju* (floating rice wine). Recently, restaurants specializing in *pajeon* have proliferated with the revived popularity of *makgeolli* (Korean rice wine).

A Dish to Share with Friends

Because green onions are rich in vitamins and minerals, and seafood has a high protein and calcium content, *pajeon* is a dish that provides a balanced nutrition all by itself. The savory smell and crispy texture make for a mouth-watering treat. *Pajeon* tastes even more delicious when shared with friends. The moment a sizzling *pajeon* arrives at the table, everyone digs in with their chopsticks and finishes the plate in no time. The anxious wait for the next one is all part of the fun. Preparing *pajeon* is also fun—pouring the mixture into the pan, pressing down with a spatula, waiting until the edges turn crispy and golden brown, and flipping it over with style.

Perfect on a Rainy Day

For some reason, people associate rain with *pajeon*. Some say it's because the sound of raindrops hitting the ground or a window sill reminds people of sizzling and spattering oil. This theory may not be totally groundless. According to an experiment conducted by the Sound Engineering Research Lab of Soongsil University, the two sounds have almost identical vibrations and frequencies. There is another physiological explanation: rain increases the discomfort index and decreases blood sugar levels. In response to these changes, the human body naturally craves foods made from starchy wheat flour. A more layman's view would be that, on a wet, cold day, people simply crave for food that will warm and comfort them.

Dongrae-pajeon

The most famous *pajeon* is *dongrae-pajeon*. Dongrae is a hot springs town in the Busan area, located in between Eonyang, an area famous for *minari* (Korean parsley), *jjokpa* (green scallion), a fishing town with plentiful seafood. *Dongrae-pajeon* is cooked in the following way. Line up thin green onion stems on a cast-iron griddle. Place five or six different kinds of seafood over the scallions. Cover with another layer of green onions and Korean parsley. Let the vegetables cook while intermittently spooning hot oil over them. Pour a batter made of ground rice—half sweet and half regular rice—followed by beaten eggs to coat the pancake and add color. *Dongrae-pajeon* is unrivaled in terms of portion size and taste. This cooking method has become the most popular way for making *pajeon*, and *dongrae-pajeon* and has become synonymous with *pajeon* itself.

The Commoners' Feast
Bindae-tteok

[Mung Bean Pancake]

Made with ground mung beans, pork, mung bean sprouts, and fiddleheads, *bindae-tteok* has a savory flavor and a crispy crunch. For an ideal cake with crunchy edges and a moist center, it should be shallow-fried with on a griddle over low heat.

Alms for the Poor in Famine Years

Bindae-tteok is also called *binja-tteok*. There are many stories on the origin of the dish. According to one, a *bindae-tteok* was a small griddlecake used as a prop to support the towering piles of pan-fried meats placed on the ancestral rites table, or *gyojasang* (large traditional Korean dining table). As this griddlecake became a commonly eaten food among the poor, it became known as *binja-tteok* (*binja* refers to the poor) and grew in size. Another story has it that in the old days, Jeongdong, a district of Seoul, was nicknamed Bindaegol for its plentiful *bindae* (bedbugs). Coincidentally, a number of *binja-tteok* sellers lived along its streets. In this version of the story, *binja-tteok* started to be called *bindae-tteok*, the compound of *bindae* from *bindaegol* and *tteok* from *binja-tteok*. There is also a theory that *bindae-tteok* originated from *bingjeo*, a pan-fried mung bean dish. Over time, *bingjeo* changed into *bingja-tteok*, and then *binja-tteok*, and finally settled as *bindae-tteok*. It is well known that in the Joseon era, in years following a bad harvest, influential families prepared *bindae-tteok* and handed them out to the poor homeless people gathered around Namdaemun (South Gate) in Seoul, crying out "Alms from a certain family!"

A Nutritious Fatigue Reliever

With its golden brown color and savory aroma, a slice of piping hot *bindae-tteok* delights the palate. As a popular song reminds us with the line "If you don't have money, just go home and cook yourself some *bindae-tteok*," this mung bean griddlecake was once regarded as a dish mainly eaten by the poor. It was especially popular in the northwestern regions of Korea. The dish, which was often cooked for guests, has become a favorite side dish for drinks. Mung beans, the main ingredient of *bindae-tteok*, are nutritious: it is rich in iron and carotene, and helps detoxify the body. When you feel physically or psychologically worn out, eating *bindae-tteok* is a great way to revive the spirit and boost energy.

Bindae-tteok tastes much better when enjoyed after dipping in soy sauce mixed with spring onions, garlic, crushed roasted sesame seeds, and other flavorings.

A Delicacy Made of Aged Sour Kimchi
Kimchi-jeon
[Kimchi Pancake]

Kimchi-jeon is an easy dish that can be prepared simply by pan-frying chopped kimchi mixed into a flour batter. For an even more special *kimchi-jeon*, one or two additional ingredients can be added to the mix, such as ground pork or chopped squid, which both pair well with kimchi.

A Dish for Many

The joy of serving *jeon* (pan-fried delicacies) lies in the instantaneous response from those who eat them. Although, as with other foods, *jeon* is especially delicious when eaten in company, it is particularly fun for a group to share *kimchi-jeon* together on a rainy day. As soon as a piping hot *kimchi-jeon* is served, it is descended upon and torn apart with chopsticks or fingers. To provide a savory accent to *kimchi-jeon*, season the chopped kimchi ahead of time. Moreover, when mixing the batter, using kelp broth instead of water gives it an even deeper flavor. *Kimchi-jeon* has enjoyed enormous popularity in other countries, especially in Japan, ever since it was introduced in *A Journey in Search of Korea's Beauty*, a travel photo essay authored by Bae Yong Joon, a famous Korean actor and a leader of the Hallyu, or Korean Wave (a boom in Korean pop culture in overseas countries). It is said that *kimchi-jeon* was featured in a variety of TV programs targeting ethnic Koreans abroad.

The perfect treat for a rainy day, crispy, and nicely-textured *kimchi-jeon* becomes even tastier with the addition of kimchi liquid to a flour batter blended with well-ripened kimchi.

For Sharing on Joyous Occasions
Modum-jeon
[Assorted Savory Pancakes]

Jeon (pan-fried delicacies) can be made from meat, fish, shellfish, or vegetables seasoned with salt and black pepper and dipped in a flour and egg batter before being pan-fried golden brown. *Jeon* is a familiar yet still very special dish among Koreans.

A Healthy, Tasty All-time Favorite

On holidays such as *seol* (New Year's Day) or *chuseok* (fall harvest festival), as well as on feast days celebrating special occasions, the Koreans of the past constructed a temporary oven by stacking rocks in the corner of the yard, set a cauldron lid over this stove, and cooked *jeon*. With the exception of the cauldron lid, things haven't changed all that much. Korean people still prepare *jeon* for special events. Indeed, as a holiday draws near, Korean TV home shopping channels feature specialized electric frying pans designed to cook a large number of *jeon* at the same time. The beauty of *jeon* is that it preserves the natural flavor of the ingredients without complex seasoning or sauces. In addition, traditional pan-frying makes food tasty without the excess oil of deep-fried dishes. *Jeon*, especially *modum-jeon*, is a good one-dish-meal that isn't too heavy but pleasantly filling. As a matter of fact, in overseas Korean restaurants, *jeon* is often the default dish of choice, much like the popular steak of western restaurants.

Koreans have long enjoyed a wide array of *jeon* thanks to the abundance of so many different seasonal ingredients. Any hot *jeon*, freshly cooked to a golden brown and briefly dipped in savory soy sauce, is beyond comparison.

HOE
[Sliced Raw Fish or Meat]

Koreans have a long history of enjoying *hoe*. Fish is sometimes eaten raw as *saengseon-hoe*, but meat is also enjoyed parboiled as *yuk-hoe*, or seasoned and mixed with various vegetables as *hoe-muchim*. Fresh, raw beef is julienned and seasoned to create a Korean-style beef steak tartare called *yuk-hoe*, a superb dish with excellent nutritional value.

The Delectable Taste of Fresh Raw Fish
Saengseon-hoe
[Sliced Raw Fish]

As a peninsula and seafaring nation, Koreans have historically eaten many sliced raw fish dishes, though perhaps not as much as the Japanese. Ancient cookbooks contain records of raw seafood dishes such as *ungeo* (Korean grenadier anchovy), *mineo* (croaker), *haesam* (sea cucumber), *jogae* (clam), *daehap* (common orient clam), and *gul* (oyster). It is said that in the summer when food tends to spoil more easily, *hoe* was eaten off a bed of ice.

Freshly Caught Fish *Hoe*

Nowadays *hoe* is dipped in a spicy vinegared red pepper paste, but before the 17th century, when chili peppers were yet to be introduced, *hoe* was dipped in mustard and vinegar soy sauce. There are two types of *saengseon-hoe* based on the color of the fish flesh: red and white. White-flesh fish such as *neopchi* (olive flounder), *ureok* (rockfish), *dom* (sea bream) or *nongeo* (sea bass) are considered high-quality ingredients for *hoe*. It is because being firmer in texture than red-flesh fish such as *bangeo* (yellowtail), *chamchi* (tuna), or *godeungeo* (mackerel), they provide a wonderful chewing experience. Most Japanese sashimi is made from aged raw fish: raw fish is usually left to age for a certain time before it is consumed. In comparison, most Koreans prefer the chewy texture of freshly caught fish.

Mak-hoe, Sekkosi and *Gwamegi*

Mak-hoe is a platter of roughly cut chunks of raw fish eaten with a *makjang* (fast-fermented soybean paste) dip or served on a bed of shredded vegetables to be mixed with *makjang*. Those who lived by the sea during their childhood talk about still finding *mak-hoe* more appetizing than the uniform *saengseon-hoe* slices: they cannot forget the fresh taste of fish sliced immediately after being caught from the sea.

While a horrifying sight to some foreigners, eating wriggling bits of *sannakji-hoe* (live common octopus cut and served immediately) is an all-time favorite treat in Korea. An even more strange sight is that of someone eating *sebalnakji-hoe* which is only for the adventurous gourmet. The *sebalnakji* (baby octopus with thin tentacles) is held by the head, the tentacles straightened out with the fingers, and devoured whole.

Another *hoe* cherished by Koreans is *sekkosi*, or slices of small fishes with the bone in. Though no longer available now, traditionally Busan locals enjoyed whale meat *hoe* and Pohang people enjoyed *gwamegi* (freeze-dried Pacific herring) as drink accompaniments. Due to a shortage of herring, the original ingredient for *gwamegi*, nowadays mackerel pike is often used in its stead. Mackerel pike is dried by sea breeze, and then the semi-stiffened flesh is cut, topped with thinly sliced scallion and sea mustard, and served with a *gochujang* dipping sauce.

Savory Morsels that Melt in the Mouth

Yuk-hoe

[Beef Tartare]

Yuk-hoe consists of a mound of thin, seasoned, and julienned lean fresh uncooked beef. It is indigenous to Korea and not found in neighboring Japan or China. A lean prime cut of beef is sliced thin and seasoned with soy sauce, minced garlic, sesame seeds, and sugar. Adding sliced pear into the mix will result in a savory taste that is hard to forget.

Meat Lovers' Choice of Meat

Koreans have long enjoyed various types of meat as *yuk-hoe*. Thinly julienned beef is of course the most common ingredient of *yuk-hoe*, but various parts such as beef kidney, liver, and omasum (*cheonyeop*) are also mixed with the same seasoning to make what is called *gap-hoe*. *dongchi-hoe* is *yuk-hoe* made with raw pheasant meat. Traditionally, pheasants were slaughtered in the winter, gutted, and left to freeze on ice or snow. Then the hardened flesh was cut into thin slices and marinated with vinegar soy sauce, ginger, and scallion.

The Light Taste of Fresh Lean Beef

One taste of *yuk-hoe* is enough to convert anyone with a prejudice against eating raw beef. Many people who think uncooked meat will be tough are in for a pleasant surprise. Because meat protein immediately coagulates when cooked over heat, cooked meat is tough unless there's sufficient marbling, but *yuk-hoe* is both lean and tender. The meat seems to melt as soon as it touches the tongue, filling the mouth with a light yet wonderful flavor. The sliced pear served with *yuk-hoe* contains digestive enzymes that tenderize the meat, which is why pear juice is often used for marinating *bulgogi* and *galbi*.

The True Taste of Beef

The most recent trend in beef *hoe* dishes is to eat it plain with minimal seasoning: cuts of lean beef are chopped into bite-sized bits and dipped in a simple salt and sesame oil sauce or vinegared red pepper paste sauce. Originally, this was how *yuk-hoe* was prepared in the Jeolla Provinces, where many households raised cattle, but it has now become popular nationwide for being the best way to enjoy the unique flavor of fresh beef.

A Nose-clearing, Eye-watering Delicacy
Hongeo-hoe
[Sliced Raw Skate]

Hongeo-hoe is fermented raw skate served with vinegared red pepper paste (*gochujang*) sauce or seasoned soy sauce. Aged kimchi can also be served on the side to wrap the bite-sized *hoe* slices. Thinly sliced *hongeo-hoe* can be mixed with Korean parsley and vinegared *gochujang*, resulting in a spicy salad. In the Jeolla Provinces, no matter how many delicacies are served, no feast can be truly complete without a pungent plate of *hongeo-hoe*.

Addictive *Hongeo-hoe*: One Bite Is Never Enough

Many people who have never tried *hongeo-hoe* think of it as a dare, repulsed by its unique and pungent smell. Yet the taste is heavenly, and one bite is said to be enough to get one addicted. Gourmets have even ranked the parts of *hongeo-hoe*, and the winner was without contention the skate's glossy, slimy nose. People will say that you are not qualified to discuss the taste of *hongeo* if you haven't tasted it. Placing a piece of *hongeo* nose, dipped in salt, in one's mouth results in an immediate stinging sensation that starts at the tongue, climbs up the nose, and finally makes the eyes swell with tears. The sensation is hard to describe and could be a numbing experience for first timers. The part voted in second place was the wing, and the third was the tail. Both parts are enjoyed for their soft and crunchy texture.

The Stronger the Smell of Ammonia, the Better the *Hongeo-hoe*

Skate caught fresh in the waters surrounding Heuksan Island in South Jeolla Province are the most valued, but the best places to eat fermented skate are the nearby cities of Mokpo and Naju. Residents of Heuksan Island prefer *hongeo-hoe* made with unfermented skate. Fermenting skate is a complex process. In the past, the skate was sometimes wrapped in hemp or rice straw and covered in compost in order to accelerate fermentation with the heat. The smell of fermented skate is not the result of rotting, but because of the ammonia that is produced while bacteria grow during the fermentation process.

The famous *samhap* is a dish that slices the fermented skate skin and seasons it with a sweet and spicy sauce, and serves it with 3 year-old aged kimchi and boiled pork. This dish is the famous *samhap*, or "medley of three." On its own, *hongeo-hoe* can be served with a simple vinegared *gochujang* sauce, mustard soy sauce, or chili powder with salt. The beverage that best accompanies *hongeo-hoe* is *makgeolli* (Korean rice wine) because it softens the stinging taste and strong smell of the *hongeo*. *Hongeo-hoe* can be mixed a heap of Korean parsley (*minari*) and seasoning to make *hongeo-hoe-muchim*. In this case, the *hongeo-hoe* is first immersed in *makgeolli* vinegar and then drained of excess liquid, to preserve the soft and crunchy texture.

KIMCHI

[Kimchi]

The characteristic that best defines Korean cuisine is the use of fermentation as a cooking method. Kimchi is a uniquely Korean creation made with a main vegetable that is first pickled in salt to draw out excess water, then mixed with other vegetables and *jeotgal* and left to ferment. Rich in vitamins, minerals, dietary fiber, and lactobacillus, kimchi is a healthy pickle when consumed in moderation.

Satisfying with Every Meal
Baechu-kimchi
[Kimchi]

Baechu-kimchi is made by stuffing salted napa cabbages (*baechu*) with a mixture of julienned white radish, red chili pepper powder, minced garlic, chopped scallion, salted seafood (*jeot-gal*) other ingredients. Kimchi, along with a bowl of steamed rice, is an essential part of every Korean meal. When consumed in moderation, kimchi has various health benefits, and, as the most well-known and familiar Korean dish to foreigners.

A Traditional Dish with 1,500 Years of History

Kimchi is a fermented dish made with vegetables and a variety of seasoning ingredients. There are currently over three hundred varieties, but when it was first made prior to the Three Kingdoms Period (57-668AD), making kimchi required a very simple recipe of salting and storing napa cabbages in an earthenware vessel to ferment for some time.

In the old days, kimchi was an important source of vitamins in the winter when fresh vegetables are unavailable. What was originally a simple salted pickle now requires various seasonings, but the modernization of the kimchi-making process has allowed it to become well known throughout the world. kimchi varies by climate, geographical conditions, local ingredients, methods of preparation and preservation.

Kimchi as an Ingredient for *Jjigae* and Fried Rice

In the cold northern regions, kimchi is mild and made with less salt or chili powder, and is more watery. It is also sliced in larger pieces. Salted shrimp or yellow croaker is usually added as *jeotgal*. In the warmer south, however, more salt, *jeotgal* and chili powder are added for preservation purposes, resulting in spicier, saltier, and drier kimchi. Kimchi is low in calories, high in dietary fiber and vitamins A, B, and C. The protein-rich *jeotgal* provides amino acids, which helps kimchi balance the carbohydrate-based Korean diet of rice. After around ten days of aging, *baechu-kimchi* ripens and acquires a crisp and tangy taste. While *baechu-kimchi* is delicious in itself, it also serves as an ingredient for various dishes. Kimchi pot stew made with *mugeun-kimchi* (kimchi aged for over a year) and chunks of fatty pork is irresistible. Kimchi can be stir-fried with rice, and kimchi liquid can be used as a sauce to mix with noodles or rice.

Geotjeori: Freshly-seasoned Kimchi
Geotjeori is napa cabbage mixed with a seasonings and spices right before it is served and eaten like a fresh salad. Foreigners, who are not used to the taste of fermented *baechu-kimchi*, will find *geotjeori* easier to enjoy. An extra spicy version of *geotjeri* is a must with *kalguksu* (handcut noodle soup) or *sujebi* (Korean pasta soup).

Simple Colors and Clean Taste
Baek-kimchi

[White Kimchi]

Baek-kimchi is made without adding red chili powder. Even until the 20th century, whole *baechu-kimchi* and *baek-kimchi* were not unlike each other: only the former contained red chili powder, and the latter, thin slices of fresh red chili peppers. To enhance the clean taste of *baek-kimchi*, salted shrimp should be the only *jeotgal* (salted seafood) used if any, and the liquid should be strained several times.

A Mild Taste Loved by Men and Women of All Ages

The original kimchi was a type of *baek-kimchi*. As red chili powder was introduced to Korea after the Japanese Invasion in 1592, Koreans began making spicy kimchi. But that did not mean the end of white kimchi. Instead, expensive ingredients such as pear, pine nuts, jujubes, chestnuts, oysters were added and it evolved into a higher quality kimchi. *Baek-kimchi* ripens and sours faster than kimchi which contains red chili powder. And because of its mild taste, *baek-kimchi* is good for the elderly, young children, or patients who should avoid overly spicy foods. It is also good for foreigners who don't want their kimchi too spicy.

Health Benefits of *Baechu*
Baechu (napa cabbage) is an excellent source of dietary fiber with a bounty of calcium and vitamin C. The dietary fiber found in *baechu* helps stimulate intestinal activity, easing bowel movements.

Crisp Slices in a Cold, Refreshing Liquid
Nabak-kimchi
[Water Kimchi]

Nabak-kimchi is a watery kimchi that contains napa cabbage and white radish slices as its main ingredients. It is usually served in the spring, but the fresh taste can be enjoyed in any season. *Nabak-kimchi* is placed on the table for ancestral rites, and served with *tteokguk* (rice cake soup) for the first meal of each Lunar New Year. Because retaining the freshness is essential to a good *nabak-kimchi*, wealthy families were said to have made it every other day.

The Perfect Kimchi to Eat with Rice Cakes

Nabak-kimchi means kimchi made with square-cut vegetables ("Na-bak-Na-bak" adds to the verb, "to cut," the meaning, "into squares"), but it could also mean kimchi made with white radish, considering that white radish was once called "*nabok.*" *Nabak-kimchi* is not only served with regular meals, but is also with snacks such as rice cakes, *mandu* (dumplings), *yaksik* (sweet rice with nuts and jujubes), or other sweets. This is because the fresh tangy liquid stimulates the palate, and the digestive enzymes in the white radish calm the stomach. Kimchi liquid is sometimes used in the broths for *guksumari* or *naengmyeon* (wheat or buckwheat noodles in cold broth), but it is especially good to wash down sticky rice cake pieces. The "kimchi soup" in the saying, "drinking kimchi soup before getting any rice cakes," refers to the liquid of *nabak-kimchi.*

Differences between *Nabak-kimchi* and *Dongchimi*

Nabak-kimchi and *dongchimi* are watery varieties of kimchi made with radish. *Dongchimi* is prepared purely with radishes and can be stored and consumed over long periods, whereas *nabak-kimchi* is created with the addition of thin green onions (*jjokpa*), apple, and pear in order to slightly sweeten the liquid. The fact that *nabak-kimchi* has to be consumed right when it is made also separates it from *dongchimi*. Red chili pepper powder is added to the *nabak-kimchi* liquid to enhance its refreshing taste.

Dongchimi
Dongchimi is a radish water kimchi mainly intended for winter storage. Its clean and refreshing liquid is used in broths for noodles or *naengmyeon* and it is also often served as a complement to rice cake or steamed sweet potato.

The Perfect Relish for *Seolleong-tang* or *Gomtang*
Kkakdugi
[Diced Radish Kimchi]

Kkakdugi is a kimchi made by salting white radish cubes, draining excess water, then season-ing the cubes with red chili pepper powder, salted shrimp, Korean parsley, minced garlic, and scallion. When *seolleong-tang* (ox bone soup) started gaining international popularity, so did *kkakdugi*, the kimchi that is served with *seolleong-tang*.

Suk-kkakdugi and *Jeong-kkakdugi*

Gukbap (rice in soup) tastes best when sour *kkakdugi* liquid is stirred into the broth. *Kkakdugi* also goes especially well with meat-based soups such as *seolleong-tang* or *gomtang* (thick beef soup), because the sour kimchi liquid reduces the greasiness of the meat stock. Since ancient times, kimchi has been prepared with great care, using different methods to suit the needs of different people. This was also the case with *kkakdugi*. For elderly people with weak teeth, gums, and digestive systems, *suk-kkakdugi*, a softer version of *kkakdugi* made with white radish softened by pre-boiling and mixed with finely-chopped salted shrimp. Pregnant women were given *jeong-kkakdugi*, where the radish was cut into perfect cubes to express the wish for a healthy, perfect baby.

Radishes contain saccharides, amino acids, minerals, and amylase while boasting seven times the vitamin C of apples. Shredded radish or radish juice, with its pungent and peppery flavor, is rich in compounds that are believed to aid in cancer prevention and enhance stomach function.

A Crunchy Cucumber Delight

Oi-sobagi
[Cucumber Kimchi]

Oi-sobagi is a kimchi made by making cross-shaped slits in cucumber pieces, and stuffing it with a seasoned mixture of chives, garlic, and red chili powder. In the past, *oi-sobagi* was eaten in the hot summer when people lost their appetites. But nowadays, with cucumbers available all year round, *oi-sobagi* has become seasonless.

A Cooling, Appetizing Summer Kimchi

Cucumbers have high water content and known to cool the body. Meanwhile, chives are known to have a warming effect. Thus the two perfectly compliment each other when used as ingredients for *oi-sobagi*. Another cucumber treat is *oiji* (salted cucumber), which is made by stacking cucumbers in a earthenware crock, sprinkling with salt, and pouring boiled, salt water over them. *Oiji* is salty yet also refreshing and makes a great summer side dish. Seasoning sliced *oiji* with chili powder, minced scallion, crushed garlic and sesame oil will give you *oiji-muchim* (seasoned salted cucumber) which has a soft and crunchy texture. It goes especially well with a bowl of steamed rice mixed in cold water.

For anyone who craves a refreshing treat during a long, stifling hot spell, cucumber is a perfect snack for its refreshing taste and crunchy texture. This vegetable is ideal for hikers, as it slakes both thirst and hunger.

Health Benefits of Garlic Chives
Garlic chives (*buchu*), a supplementary ingredient in *oi-sobagi*, are known to be effective in preventing colds. Their aryl radical substances help stimulate digestion and strengthen the intestines, while providing energy boosting effects as well.

MIT-BANCHAN

[Basic Side Dishes]

Namul—vegetables and greens which are harvested in the fields and mountainsides — is a unique side dish that can only be found in Korea. There are two main types of *namul*: *saengchae* made by dressing fresh vegetables, and *sukchae* prepared by first blanching or boiling the ingredients. The base ingredients for *namul* are full of healthy vitamins and minerals. *Jangajji* and *jeotgal* are also uniquely Korean fermented pickles, each with a flavor of its own depending on the ingredients and method of fermentation.

A True Health Food for Everyone
Namul
[Seasoned Vegetables]

Namul includes all the side dishes made from vegetables, greens, herbs, or wild roots harvested in the mountains and in the fields. It is also a general term for any type of edible plant ingredient. *Namul* includes both *saengchae* and *sukchae* but mostly refers to *sukchae*. Vegetables, mushrooms, or sprouts can all be used to make *namul*.

Rich in Vitamins and Minerals

There are as many, if not more, varieties of *namuls* as salads. To name just a few: julienned and sautéed *mu-namul* (radish *namul*); thinly sliced, salted, rinsed, drained, and sautéed *oi-namul* (cucumber *namul*); blanched and seasoned *cham-namul* (Pimpinella brachycarpa, a wild green *namul*), *kkaennip-namul* (perilla leaf *namul*), and *gochunnip-namul* (pepper leaf *namul*). No wonder there's an old saying "As long as you remember 99 names of *namul*, you will never starve." Korea is a mountainous country blessed with plenty of sunshine, so wild greens and vegetables can easily be found growing all over the mountains and fields. Even though some vegetables are seasonal, most can be dried and used whenever needed, just with some soaking and boiling.

There are two main recipes for preparing *namul*: stir-frying with oil and seasoning, or just mixing the seasoning with the pre-cooked ingredient. The seasoning is usually comprised of soy sauce, ground roasted sesame seeds, chopped scallion and garlic. Vinegar, by principle, is not used. Salt is used instead of soy sauce if one desires to preserve the color and delicate taste of the ingredients. In the old days, ground pine nuts were occasionally used in place of ground roasted sesame seeds.

Stir-fried *Namul* and Blanched *Namul*

Popular ingredients for cooked *namul* include osmund ferns, bracken fiddleheads, bellflower, mushrooms, aster leaves, dried radish leaves, cucumber, summer squash, and aubergines. To make *namul*, vegetables or greens are stir-fried with oil and then seasoned with soy sauce, scallion, garlic, and ground roasted sesame seeds. Sometimes, julienned and seasoned beef is stir-fried together with the vegetables. Ingredients for blanched *namuls* include spinach, crown daisy, Korean parsley, mung bean sprouts, and bean sprouts. After blanching, excess liquid is squeezed out and the vegetables are mixed with oil, soy sauce, ground roasted sesame seeds, scallion, and garlic. The liquid is squeezed out to prevent the *namul* from becoming soggy and bland. A few different types of *namul* are usually placed together on the same plate for an attractive presentation, but fresh and sautéed *namuls* are usually put on separate plates. Several different *namuls* can be arranged on a single plate to combine different flavors and create a contrast between colors, e.g. white *namul* versus green *namul*.

The Universe in Nine Compartments
Gujeol-pan
[Platter of Nine Delicacies]

Gujeol-pan refers to a Korean specialty made up of eight different kinds of vegetables and meats placed in the outer eight sections of an octagonal wooden serving dish and thin wheat crepes stacked in the central compartment. The term *gujeol-pan* literally means "nine-sectioned wooden plate," which also serves as the name of the dish.

A Work of Art

It is commonly said that the taste of Chinese dishes is determined by the fire, Japanese dishes by the knife, and Korean dishes by the hand. *Gujeol-pan* is an elaborate dish which best demonstrates the detailed and painstaking work that goes into the preparation. A *gujeol-pan* container is typically made of lacquered wood, while more elaborate versions are inlaid with mother-of-pearl. The eight outer sections are filled with an assortment of meats and vegetables, while the center is usually reserved for the wheat crepe wraps which can also be tinted in subtle colors. The assembled dish is a true work of culinary art and never fails to impress the guests.

Meat, Vegetables, and Even Nuts

People eating *gujeol-pan* take the fillings of their choice, place them on the wheat crepe, wrap, and eat. This task can be a challenge to those less skilled with chopsticks. For this reason, the crepes are sometimes wrapped with fillings beforehand and served on a plate. The tangy taste of the dipping sauce made of mustard, vinegar, and soy sauce provides a pleasant twist to this dish.

Gujeol-pan is also used as serving dish in a *juansang* (a table with wine and side dishes) or *dagwasang* (a table with refreshments). For *juansang*, the *gujeol-pan* is filled with dry foods that go well with wine, such as raw chestnuts, walnuts, ginkgo nuts, jujubes, pine nuts, peanuts, and dried persimmons. With *dagwasang*, several kinds of *gangjeong* (deep-fried sweet rice puffs), *jeonggwa* (candied fruits or roots), *dasik* (tea confectionery), and *suksilgwa* (glazed fruits and nuts) are placed in a colorful arrangement. Together, these two presentations are called *geon-gujeol-pan* (*gujeol-pan* with dry snacks).

Mil-jeonbyeong, a Product of Great Craft and Skill

Mil-jeonbyeong, or wheat crepes, are not easy to prepare. They are made by combining wheat flour and water, then pouring the batter into a pan in round shapes. Once cooked, the crepes are carefully removed using a wooden skewer, and trimmed to fit the central compartment of the *gujeol-pan*. The pan must be wiped of excess oil before the batter is poured, the heat must be very low, and the resulting crepes must be paper-thin. These often remind people of the "crêpe," a classic French dish also well known to Koreans.

Pearl Buck and *Gujeol-pan*

There is a well-known story that cannot be left out when talking about *gujeol-pan*. The story is about the Nobel Prize-winning author Pearl S. Buck, who was invited to a meal during a visit to South Korea. At the center of the table was a black, octagonal lacquer box. When Ms. Buck lifted the lid, she discovered nine different foods arranged by color, creating a striking and beautiful harmony while contrasting against the black lid. Although delighted with the beauty of the dish, Ms. Buck refused to touch it, saying that she couldn't destroy such a work of art by eating it.

A Low-fat Dish Perfect for Dieting
Dotori-muk
[Acorn Jelly Salad]

Dotori-muk is considered an ideal food for dieters, because it allows diners to feel full with a minimum amount of calories, thanks to its high water content. The tannins in the acorn leave a slightly bitter aftertaste, which also prevents people from eating large portions. All combined, it makes for a perfect dish for those looking to shed some extra pounds.

A Dish for a King in Wartime

Dotori, or acorns, have been consumed since the Stone Age, as demonstrated by the widespread discovery of wild acorns at archeological sites. There is a story related to the oak trees that produce the acorns. King Seonjo of the Joseon Dynasty was forced to flee the royal palace and head for the northern regions to escape the Japanese Invasion of 1592. At that time, in the northern part of Korea, oak trees were called *tori-namu*. Since the war was raging, there was little to eat, but the people of the village where the king was residing felt compelled to serve their king. They prepared a jelly from acorn starch, what they called "*torimuk*," and served it to the king. The hungry monarch devoured the acorn jelly with great relish. After he returned to the royal palace, in order to remind himself of this period of hardship, he ordered that "*torimuk*" be served. *Torimuk* thus became an important and regular part of the royal meal, and since then, *dotori*, or acorns, was also called *sangsuri*, meaning food placed on the king's table.

The Legend of Bakdaljae

There is a popular song whose lyrics mention *dotori-muk*: "wul-go-neom-neun-bak-dal-jae" which can be translated as "Bakdaljae that can't be passed without tears." Bakdaljae is a name of a hill in Pyeongdong-ri, Jecheon, North Chungcheong Province, the origin of the sorrowful legend of Bakdal and Keumbong. On his way to Hanyang—the ancient name for Seoul—to take the civil service examination, a young man named Bakdal stopped in Pyeongdong-ri to pass the night. He happened to meet and fell in love with a maiden named Keumbong. The two promised themselves to one another, but they were forced to part when Bakdal had to finally leave for the examination. Keumbong waited for three months and ten days, but heard not a word from Bakdal. Driven to despair, Keumbong eventually died of a broken heart. After failing the examination, Bakdal returned to Pyeongdong-ri, but arrived too late to save Keumbong. He ended up throwing himself off a cliff upon hearing of Keumbong's death. The food Keumbong had prepared for Bakdal when he was about to leave for Hanyang was *dotori-muk*, hence the lyric "Packing *dotori-muk* for Bakdal, at Bakdaljae, Keumbong never stops crying." It is historically accurate that *dotori-muk* was carried on long journeys, because it does not easily spoil.

Crispy and Refreshing
Oi-seon
[Stuffed Cucumber]

Originally, *oi-seon* was a Korean royal dish prepared by stuffing cucumbers with meat filling, steaming them and then pouring chilled *jangguk* (clear beef broth) over them. It was originally cooked over a slow fire, but to better suit the modern preference for a more refreshing and crunchy texture, lightly fried cucumbers are slit, stuffed with sautéed meat and *jidan* (egg garnish) and then dressed with a sweet and sour vinegar sauce.

A Vinegary Summer Delicacy

In the royal cuisine, the term *seon* refers to traditional dishes prepared by steaming vegetables or fish that have been stuffed or mixed with meat. The vegetables used to make *seon* dishes included cucumbers, summer squash, aubergine, tofu, and napa cabbage. Among these *seon* dishes, *oi-seon* is suitable as a summer dish because of its fresh fragrance and clear green color. These days, cucumbers are usually eaten uncooked. In the past, however, they were used as ingredients in *gochujang-jjigae* (hot pepper paste pot stew), as well as pan-fried or steamed dishes. When cucumbers are added to *jjigae* (pot stew), the broth becomes refreshing and the cucumber bits remain crunchy even after cooking. The bite-sized cucumber pieces lined in a row compose a beautiful plate, and for this reason it is frequently served as an appetizer when entertaining guests. Although finely slicing the ingredients can be quite laborious, it is certainly worth the effort.

Cucumber as a Beauty Aid

Cucumber is 95 percent water. It is an alkaline food rich in potassium and vitamin C. In China, it was said that cucumbers make women beautiful, and that beautiful women smelled of a cucumber-like fragrance. For this reason, some Chinese women would carry a cucumber hidden in their bosoms. *Oi-seon* is made with vitamin-rich cucumbers, sautéed meat, *pyogo* mushrooms (shiitake), and *jidan* (egg garnish) to create a nutritious food packed with essential amino acids.

Dubu-seon and Eo-seon
Oi-seon, dubu-seon, and *eo-seon* were frequently served at the royal court during the Joseon Dynasty era. *Dubu-seon* is made by mincing tofu, squeezing out the excess water, adding ground chicken meat, and then forming it into shapes. Garnished with sliced shiitake and black mushrooms, it is then steamed. When decorated with a garnish of red chili pepper threads and pine nuts, it appears all the more beautiful. After cooling, it is sliced and served with a blend of soy sauce, vinegar and mustard. *Eo-seon* refers to steamed fish stuffed with sautéed beef and vegetables.

Seasoned with Love
Japchae
[Stir-fried Glass Noodles and Vegetables]

Japchae is made by boiling glass noodles, draining, and mixing them with stir-fried spinach, carrots, mushrooms, beef, and onions. It is both a special dish and a versatile favorite. It has been chosen as one of the most popular Korean dishes in the world, along with *bulgogi*, *galbi-gui*, and *bibimbap*.

A Classic Dish on Festive Days

No Korean festivity is complete without *japchae*. It has long been perceived as a luxurious and elegant dish and was always served on birthdays, weddings, and 60th birthday celebrations. *Japchae* was first created in the 17th century when King Gwanghaegun hosted a palace banquet. The *Gwanghaegun ilgi* (Daily Records of King Gwanghaegun's Reign) records that Yi Chung, one of the king's favorites, had the habit of personally presenting unusual dishes to the king. Gwanghaegun relished these dishes so much that he would not start a meal until they arrived. Among these, it was *japchae* that most captivated the heart of the king. Traditional *japchae* was made purely with vegetables, lacking the glass noodles that characterize the current style of *japchae*. It was also recorded that thinly-sliced and sautéed vegetables would be placed in a plate and topped with a special sauce, along with Sichuan pepper, black pepper, and ginger powder. The special sauce was concocted by combining pheasant broth, strained soybean paste and wheat flour, and then reducing it to a thick consistency.

Old-style *Japchae* without Glass Noodles

The term *japchae* is a combination of *jap*, meaning "mix, gather, or plentiful" and *chae*, meaning "vegetables." Thus, it can be translated as "assorted mixed vegetables." The current form of *japchae* made with glass noodles became common after a *dangmyeon* (glass noodles made from sweet potato starch) factory was first erected in Sariwon in 1919. It became popular only after 1930.

In 2009, former first lady Kim Yoon-ok made *japchae* during a CNN interview, drawing considerable attention. Ms. Kim invited reporters from CNN to the Cheongwadae (presidential residence) and prepared *japchae*, slicing and pan-frying all the ingredients herself. Notably, when mixing the boiled glass noodles with the other ingredients, she used her hands rather than utensils to demonstrate the traditional mantra that "taste comes from the finger tips of a loving mother."

Boiled glass noodles may swell if left unattended for too long. So, in order to prepare a large batch of *japchae*, the glass noodles can simply be steeped in hot water instead of boiled before stir-frying.

A Dish Bestowed by the King to Stop Factional Strife
Tangpyeong-chae
[Mung Bean Jelly Salad]

Tangpyeong-chae is prepared by combining mung bean jelly with sautéed julienned beef, parboiled Korean parsley, and roasted dried laver, and is also called *cheongpomuk-muchim* (seasoned mung bean jelly). The dish, which derived its name from *tangtang-pyeongpyeong* (蕩蕩 平平), was born as a consequence of a tragic event that took place during the Joseon Dynasty.

"*Wangdo tangtang, Wangdo pyeongpyeong*"

The four main ingredients of *tangpyeong-chae* have four colors: bluish-white mung bean jelly, red beef, green Korean parsley, and black dried laver. The four colors of white, red, green, and black represented the four political factions known as the Seoin, Namin, Dongin, and Bukin. White mung bean jelly was used as the main ingredient, because the Seoin was the strongest group at the time. King Yeongjo, the 21st king of the Joseon Dynasty, was the son of King Suk-jong born by a female servant of the lowest rank in the court. When King Yeongjo succeeded his older half-brother Gyeongjong to the throne, he was accused by some of poisoning his brother. The opposing Soron faction, who had supported Gyeongjong, argued that it was not a legitimate succession.

The fact that his son, crown prince Sado, was close to the Soron sowed even further misery. Based on a misapprehension that Sado was seeking to usurp his position, King Yeongjo ended up locking up his own son in a *duiju** until he died. When the king realized what he had done, it was too late. Deeply regretting his actions, King Yeongjo implemented the Tangpyeong Policy, under which individuals were selected for government office based on merit rather than political affiliation. The term Tangpyeong was derived from a phrase in the section of the *Seokyeong** asserting, "*wangdo tangtang, wangdo pyeongpyeong*" which can be translated as "An emperor's path will be clear only when he shows no bias or favoritism towards any faction." It was a perfect phrase to demonstrate his strong resolve to never again be swayed by political factionalism. Together with the policy, King Yeongjo had a dish named *tangpyeong-chae* served to his officials as a symbol of his resolve.

Perfect Example of the Five Cardinal Colors

Korean food is often characterized by the Five Cardinal Colors, or *obangsaek*, which represent the five natural elements in yellow, blue, white, red, and black. *Obangsaek* is based on *yin* and *yang* and the "five movements" principle which says that the spirits of *yin* and *yang* gave birth to heaven and earth and then created the five elements of wood, fire, earth, metal, and water. It also refers to the five cardinal points of north, south, east, west, and center. In Korean cuisine, there are many dishes that strive to include all of the five colors. Perfect examples would be *bibimbap* and *tangpyeong-chae*.

* *Duiju* is a wooden box for the storage of grains such as rice, beans, or red beans.

* *Seokyeong* is an ancient Chinese scripture and one of the five classics of Confucianism.

Spicy, Sour, and Sweet Taste
Haepari-naengchae
[Chilled Jellyfish Salad]

Haepari-naengchae is a dish made by mixing crisp, crunchy jellyfish with an assortment of vegetables in a traditional Korean mustard sauce which is a combination of sweet and sour vinaigrette (*danchotmul*) and piquant mustard.

A Showcase of Culinary Skills

One must be careful when eating *haepari-naengchae*, as a large amount of the mustard sauce will send a sharp fume up to the nose and bring tears to the eyes. *Haepari-naengchae* is a perfect dish for entertaining guests, because the crunchy and chewy texture of jellyfish is a gastronomic treat, and the colorful dish is perfect for showing off the host's culinary skills.

A Diet and Beauty Aid

There are numerous varieties of jellyfish, but not all are suitable for cooking. Edible jellyfish is mainly caught along the coasts of Korea, China, and Japan and is primarily used in Chinese cuisine. Jellyfish can feel slippery due to mucin, a protein blend with considerable water-holding capability. Chondroitin, which makes up mucin, is a major component of skin, cartilage and blood vessels, and helps keep them supple by retaining moisture in bodily tissues. In addition, jellyfish is a low-calorie food with only 32 calories per 100 grams. Also known for its effectiveness in relieving digestive issues, it is very popular as a diet food to help treat both obesity and skin troubles.

How to Enjoy *Haepari-naengchae*
In order to get the best taste of *haepari-naengchae*, turn the salad over in the plate right before eating it. This allows you to start with the moist and well-seasoned bottom and you can fully enjoy its taste all the way through.

Salty and Savory Pickled Vegetables
Jangajji
[Pickled Vegetables]

Jangajji is vegetables pickled and ripened over a long time in salt or soy sauce. Some types of *jangajji* are made by placing vegetable pieces in soybean paste, soy sauce, fast-fermented soybean paste, or red pepper paste and left to slowly ferment.

Even Kings Relied on *Jangajji* to Cure Lost Appetites

When vegetable pieces are left for several months in a *jang* (salt brine or fermented bean paste), they absorb the *jang* flavor and can be served right out of the crock. But, more often, it is seasoned with various spices and sesame oil. Due to the saltiness of the *jangajji*, only one or two kinds of *jangajji* are enough for a meal. With the introduction of refrigerators, it has become easier to preserve foods. As a result, *jangajji* is consumed less nowadays and has been relegated to a "side dish of last resort."

However, in the old days, *jangajji* was considered a treat, even in the royal courts where it was called by the special name *janggwa*. Even the king, who was surrounded with various delicacies from the land and the sea, would sometimes lose his appetite, and on such occasions, *janggwa* would be served to stimulate his taste buds.

A Simple Accompaniment to Rice

The choice of *jang* to use for *jangajji* depends on the type of vegetable. Garlic *jangajji* is made by soaking young garlic bulbs in diluted vinegar to remove the sharp edge, and pickling them in sugared soy sauce. Using salt instead of soy sauce will result in a lighter and crispier garlic *jangajji*. The cross section of a bulb resembles a flower, and the individual cloves are crunchy and bursting with flavor. Chili pepper leaf, eggplant and sesame leaf *jangajji* are made in the same way. Tucking perilla leaves in soybean paste in autumn and taking them out to eat in early spring is called *doenjang-kkaennip-jangajji*. It has a surprising yet delightful flavor that is sharp and intense. Garlic spears and cucumbers taste best when pickled in *gochujang* (red chili pepper paste). The vegetables should be semi-dried when pickling in soybean paste or *gochujang*. When ripe, the paste is scraped off the surface of the *jangajji*, and then seasoned with sugar and sesame oil.

Tucking sesame leaves in *doenjang* (soybean paste) in autumn and leaving them over the winter, will produce pickles with a surprisingly sharp and intense flavor.

A Korea Salty "Rice Thief"
Jeotgal
[Salted Seafood]

Jeotgal is made by salting and preserving seafood. The Korean *jeotgal* has a distinctive taste which is developed in the process of salt-fermentation. Along with soybean paste, soy sauce, red pepper paste, and kimchi, *jeotgal* is one of the five basic fermented pickles in Korean cuisine. While it is sometimes served as a separate side dish to rice, *jeotgal* is also widely used to add flavor to various dishes including kimchi.

Great Variety and Wide Usage

Jeotgal made with shrimp, anchovies, and oysters are the most common types consumed as an everyday dish, but dozens of different varieties exist based on seasonal catches. Whereas fermentation in agricultural regions centered on soybeans, fishing villages created numerous *jeotgals* by fermenting the flesh and innards of fish and shellfish. Salted and fermented seafood can also be found in the cuisines of India, Vietnam, and Thailand, countries known for hot climates and an abundance of seafood, and the anchovies commonly used in Italian cuisine are also fermented. Yet no country has a richer variety of salted and fermented seafood as Korea. *Jeotgal* is intense with flavor, and served in a small amount which is plenty to finish a bowl of rice. And this is why *jeotgal* is another so-called "rice thief." The first record of *jeotgal* can be found in *Samguksagi*.* At the wedding of Silla's King Sinmun and Lady Kim, the ceremonial *pyebaek* table was set with rice, wine, oil, honey, *jang*, *meju* (fermented soybean), dried beef, and "*jeotgal*." During the Joseon period, there were largely four types of *jeotgal*: seafood fermented in salt; in a mixture of salt, liquor, oil, and Sichuan pepper; in salt and yeast; or in salt, malt, and sweet rice.

Jeotgal by Region and Season

In Korean cuisine, *jeotgal* plays an important role in defining the flavor of regional cuisines. As the ocean catches are different by region, each region has their own favorite *jeotgal* and the variety is endless. Some popular *jeotgals* that are eaten with rice include pollack roe, pollack innards, squid, and clam. Meanwhile, shrimp, anchovy, croaker, corvina, and cutlass fish *jeotgals* are mostly used as ingredients for kimchi. Making *jeotgal* may seem easy at first sight since the only process required is salt-fermentation.

However, Koreans are quite particular about their *jeotgal*, and it is not that easy considering the many different fish varieties and flavors. It is also important to keep the *jeotgal* in the right place where the temperature and humidity are ideal for fermentation. Gwangcheon salted *saeujeot* is made by fermenting salted shrimp in an underground care that maintains a temperature of 15-16°C all year long, resulting in a flavor that is famous for its subtlety and richness. As the ideal habitat of oysters is where freshwater and seawater meet, the best *eorig-ul-jeot* (seasoned oyster *jeotgal*) is produced in Ganwoldo where the river meets the Yellow Sea.

Samguksagi is the history of the three ancient Korean kingdoms of Goguryeo, Baekje, and Silla. This collection of historical records was compiled by Goryeo-era historian Kim Busik.

Crab at its Best

Ganjang-gejang

[Soy Sauce Marinated Crab]

Gejang (pickled crab), or *gejeot*, is picked whole crabs in boiled soy sauce brine. A traditional Korean dish enjoyed since before the 17th century, *ganjang-gejang* tastes best when it is made with egg-bearing crabs. Properly preserved, the roe-filled *ganjang-gejang* can be enjoyed all year round.

A Superb Combination with Rice

Gejang is only made with live crabs, which are scrubbed clean, turned upside down and drained, then placed in a container and submerged in soy sauce. Garlic cloves and whole chili peppers are thrown in for a spicier taste. Three days later, the soy sauce is drained, boiled, cooled, and poured over the crabs. After this process is repeated three to four times, the *gejang* is kept in the container ready to eat. According to *Gyuhap-chongseo,** an old collection of household advice, *gejang* was made by keeping live crabs in a crock with bits of beef overnight, and when the beef was all eaten up by the crabs, soy sauce was poured into the crock. It is said that feeding crabs with beef enhanced the taste of the crab meat. In the Jeolla Provinces, *gejang* is commonly made by chopping up live skittering sea crabs and immersing the pieces in a seasoned soy sauce for a day or two. This fresh *gejang* is called *beoltteok-gejang*, because it has to be eaten *beoltteok* (quickly) or it will go bad.

Rice in a Shell

Restaurants famous for their *ganjang-gejang* have their own soy sauce mixture that they have been using for years. Some established names even have crocks that were first filled with soy sauce over twenty years ago and never completely emptied, but only replenished once in a while. A bowl of rice vanishes in no time when eaten with *ganjang-gejang* which has achieved just the right degree of saltiness. Nevertheless, true *ganjang-gejang* enthusiasts are especially fond of a certain part: the carapace (top shell). Naturally, this does not mean that they eat the shell itself, but rice mixed in it. The combination of rice, creamy tomalley, bits of crabmeat, and crab-flavored soy sauce is so good that the taste defies description.

Gyuhap-chongseo is a home economics encyclopedia compiled by Lady Bingheogak Yi in 1809 that organizes and compiles matters related to the necessities of life.

Crab Roe *Bibimbap*

One popular dish at specialized *ganjang-gejang* houses is crab roe *bibimbap* (rice mixed with crab roe), a dish designed for those who crave *ganjang-gejang* but find it bothersome to have to pick the crab meat from its shell. The edible contents of *ganjang-gejang*, steamed rice, raw egg yolk, dried laver flakes, and sesame oil are all mixed together in a bowl. The wonderful aroma of sesame oil is what makes *ganjang-gejang* lovers choose crab roe *bibimbap* over regular *ganjang-gejang* with rice.

TTEOK, HANGWA & EUMCHEONGRYU

[Rice Cake, Korean Sweets and Beverages]

Tteok (rice cake) is filling enough to substitute rice, but it can also be a snack, as well as an essential item for banquets or ancestral rites. *Hangwa* (Korean sweets) is also deeply related to the cultural practice of ancestral rites. Korean teas and beverages are distinguished by its flavor, aroma, as well as properties that promote health and wellness. The sweet, sour, bitter, astringent, and spicy tastes all have a role in reinvigorating the body, and thus it is important to harmonize and preserve individual tastes.

Gyeongdan

Kkultteok

Yaksik

Hwajeon

Skillfully and Elaborately Prepared
Tteok
[Rice Cakes]

The old Korean expression, "*tteok* instead of *bap* (steamed rice)" implies how tasty *tteok* is. According to another old saying "No matter how much rice one eats, there is always room for *tteok*." *Tteok* was never left out on holidays or festive occasions, but it was also an everyday food made with available seasonal ingredients.

Bite-sized *Gyeongdan*

Gyeongdan refers to small balls of rice cake prepared by mixing sweet rice powder with boiling water, shaping the dough into balls about the size of chestnuts, boiling them in water, and coating them with different kinds of *gomul* (dressing powder). The small, round shape is cute, and thanks to the *gomul* preventing it from drying out, *gyeongdan* remains soft for a while. *Chalsusu-gyeongdan*, made with glutinous sorghum powder in celebration of a newborn baby's 100th day or first birthday, is coated with mashed red beans in the belief that the red color wards off evil spirits.

Sweet *Kkultteok*: One is Never Enough

In Korea, the expression *"gulttukgatta"* is commonly used to mean "eagerly wishing for something." Here *gulttuk* is derived from *kkultteok* (rice cake filled with honey). This is originally from the dialect of the Gyeongsang Provinces and is an onomatopoetic word that mimics the sound like swallowing *kkultteok*. In the past, when food was scarce, *kkultteok* was the food of dreams. The desire for *kkultteok* could be so great that when people were longing desperately for something, they used the expression *"kkultteokgatta"* to mean "I want it as much as *kkultteok*."

Yaksik: Made of Healthy Ingredients

Yaksik is a seasonal delicacy traditionally eaten on Jeongwol Daeboreum, a Korean holiday which falls on the 15th day of the first lunar month. *Yaksik* derives its name from the use of honey among its ingredients. In olden days, honey was often considered to be a medicine, which explains the word *"Yak"* meaning "medicine." Thus pan-fried *gochujang* mixed with honey was called *yakgochujang*, while deep-fried honey cookies were named *yakgwa*. Due to the healthy ingredients such as sweet rice, chestnuts, jujubes, pine nuts, and honey, *yaksik* was traditionally perceived to be a great health food.

Pan-fried *Hwajeon* Embellished with Flower Petals

Hwajeon is made by mixing sweet rice powder with boiling water, shaping the dough into small balls, arranging flower petals on top, and pan-frying them in a small amount of oil. Depending on what edible flowers are in season, *jindallae-hwajeon* was made with azaleas in the spring, *jangmi-hwajeon* with rose petals in the summer, and *gukhwajeon* with chrysanthemum flowers in the fall.

During the Joseon era, the queen would go on an outing to the Biwon Garden of Changdeok Palace on every third day of the third lunar month (Samjinnal). Alongside a stream known as the Okryucheon, round *hwajeons* would be made with sweet rice dough and decorated with azalea petals. This traditional custom was called *hwajeonnori*, literally meaning "merrymaking with *hwajeon*." Commoners also enjoyed their own *hwajeonnori*.

Gangjeong

Dasik

Yakgwa

Refined Colors, Sweet Tastes
Hangwa
[Korean Sweets]

The history of traditional Korean sweets, or *hangwa*, is deeply related to the cultural practice of ancestral rites. In seasons when no fresh fruits were available, fruit-shaped sweets were made from powdered grain and honey. The branches from these fruits were added to the dish before it was placed on ancestral rites tables. During the Joseon Dynasty, whenever a banquet was held at the royal court, confectionaries such as *gangjeong* (deep-fried honey cookies), *dasik* (tea confectionery), or *yakgwa* (deep-fried sweet rice puffs) were piled high on the banquet tables. This practice was called "*goinda*" meaning "stack up high" and an average of 24 different kinds of *hangwa* were piled as tall as 55 centimeters to create an imposing banquet table.

Crispy Crunchy *Gangjeong*

Gangjeong is notoriously difficult to make. Sweet rice powder is mixed with liquor and honey and steamed. A small amount of honey is added once again, they are cut into slices one half centimeter thick, three centimeters long and one half a centimeter wide, and then left to dry in the shade. After soaking in liquor overnight, they are dried and deep-fried in oil. Fried *gangjeongs* are coated in grain syrup and then coated with other ingredients such as beans or sesame seeds. As demonstrated by the popular phrase "hollow *gangjeong*," well-made *gangjeong* is deep-fried until it puffs up and becomes airy in the center. *Gangjeong* is naturally healthy, as it uses medicinal herbs and natural ingredients. For instance, the puffed cereal coating of *gangjeong* may be dyed pink with gromwell, yellow with pine pollen, or brown with cinnamon powder.

Sweet *Dasik* that Melts in the Mouth

Dasik is soft, sweet, and melts in the mouth. They were frequently served with tea or for dessert. *Dasik* was made with powdered rice, chestnuts or beans combined with honey or syrup and shaped in a patterned wooden mold (*dasik-pan*) into decorative forms. The shapes include a letter, flower, or geometric figure.

In the Joseon Dynasty era, *dasik* was an essential part of the table setting for special ceremonies, such as ancestral rites, weddings, and holidays. The compressed sweets also served as an emergency medicine. *Heugimja-dasik*, made with black sesame seeds, was useful for treating food poisoning, vomiting, or diarrhea. *Dotori-dasik* or acorn *dasik* were effective for suppressing coughing. *Sanyak-dasik* contained medicinal ingredients and was good for improving the health of the feeble. It was, in fact, so often served to elderly parents that they came to be called *hyoja-dasik*, meaning *dasik* for filial piety. *Dasik* is soft, sweet, and melts in the mouth. They were frequently served with tea or for dessert.

Sweet and Savory *Yakgwa*

Yakgwa refers to *yumilgwa* (deep-fried grain cookies) made with wheat flour mixed with honey and sesame oil, pressed in a *yakgwa* frame (*yakgwa-pan*), and slowly deep-fried. Afterwards, the sweets are dipped in syrup or honey to firm up the texture. According to shape, *gungjung-yakgwa* (royal court *yakgwa*) refers to an elaborate flower-shaped version molded in a *yakgwa* frame, while a bite-sized, square-shaped variety is known as *gaeseong-mo-yakgwa*. *Yakgwa* boasts a long tradition and is said to have first been made for Buddhist sacrificial rites during the United Silla period. With a soft texture and sweet flavor, it is one of the most popular sweets that children rush to eat at the end of an ancestral rite.

Green tea

Maesil tea

Yuja tea

Ginseng tea

Sweet and Soothing Aroma
Cha
[Tea]

Green tea has been savored ever since the Three Kingdoms period. Tea culture was introduced from China, flourished in Korea, and spread to Japan. Fruit tea made with sugar-preserved fruits such as *maesil* (green plum) and *yuja* (citrus) has also been popular since ancient times. However, the most famous Korean would be ginseng tea which is well-known as a tonic drink.

Green Tea, One of the World's Top Ten Health Foods

There are many theories about the origins of Korean tea culture: some say that it started when seeds were introduced from the Tang Dynasty and planted throughout the Jiri Mountain area during the Three Kingdoms period; others claim that it was introduced from India when King Kim Su-ro, the founder of Gaya Kingdom,* married a princess of the Ayutthaya Kingdom. Others assert that wild tea had been already growing throughout in the southern region.

Tea can be categorized into green tea, oolong tea or black tea, depending on the degree of fermentation. Green tea is made by roasting freshly-picked leaves. There is a special verb "deok-nen-da" meaning "to roast tea leaves" in Korean. Oolong tea is half-fermented and black tea is fully fermented. Green tea is clearly the most popular of the three. *Ujeon* tea is green tea made by roasting leaves freshly picked in the early spring, and is also known as *cheotmul* (the first infusion) tea. *Ujeon* tea is made from tender young leaves with a delicate and subtle flavor and is very expensive, since the preparation process is so difficult that only small amounts are produced.

Green tea was designated by *Time* Magazine as one of the world's top ten health foods. The catechins in green tea have been proven to be antioxidants which delay the aging of cells. Green tea is also good for the skin and weight control. Boseong in South Jeolla Province is Korea's largest producer of green tea, and its winding green tea terraces have become a famous tourist destination.

Sweet, Sour *Maesil* Tea

Maesil is the fruit of the plum tree. In early spring, clusters of small green plums can be seen hanging from the branches of trees amid the white petals. Unfortunately, there is only a brief period when green plums are available in the market. *Maesil* tea strengthens the digestive system and prevents diarrhea and constipation. It also helps cleanse the body of toxins and boosts immunity against food poisoning. Green plums produced from late May through mid-June is mixed with sugar in a one to one ratio, stored in a cool place for several months, and then strained for a sweet-and-sour fermented *maesil* syrup with a sweet aroma. This syrup can be diluted with water to one fifth its strength to make a *maesil* drink. If diluted with hot water, it becomes *maesil* tea. Add *soju*, and it becomes fragrant green plum liquor. Green plums are rich in organic acids, as well as citric acid, and break down fatigue-inducing lactic acid. It is also rich in calcium which particularly beneficial for women.

---

* Gaya Kingdom is an ancient nation in the Nakdong River basin of Southern Korea founded by King Kim Su-ro in AD 42.

Yuja Tea: Citrus for Combatting Fatigue

Yuja is an aromatic citrus fruit that is effective against arthritis and neuralgia, and also aids digestion. *Yuja-cheong*, or *yuja* syrup, is made in the same manner as *maesil* syrup, by mixing *yuja* with sugar. Most commonly, *yuja* tea is made by adding warm water to this concentrate, but *yuja* tea can also be brewed with sliced fresh *yuja* fruit or the rind. A single *yuja* fruit contains one and a half times the vitamin C of an orange and twice that of a tangerine. *Yuja* tea is consumed primarily in the wintertime as an effective relief for hangovers and also for preventing colds.

Ginseng Tea, Elixir of Immortality

The Chinese emperor Qin Shi Huang, who longed for eternal life, was known to have sent 500 couples to the shores of the Yellow Sea on a mission to obtain an herbal elixir. History tells that what was brought back was Korean ginseng. Ginseng has long been used as a general cure-all. It was mostly consumed in the form of tea which can be made from fresh ginseng (*susam*), red ginseng (*hongsam*),* and dried ginseng (*geonsam*). Sometimes, jujubes can be added for flavor. In order to make aromatic ginseng tea, ten grams of ginseng is boiled in 500 milliliters of water. Ginseng is rich in saponin which helps break down fats, aids digestion, and stimulates cellular enzymes, thus boosting the metabolism. Ginseng's anti-oxidative properties have an anti-aging effect.

---

* Red ginseng is made with a special technique of par-boiling and drying fresh ginseng. It is known to have first been produced some 1,000 years ago.

Green tea made by roasting freshly-picked leaves (upper); Green plums mixed with sugar (lower)

Sikhye

Sujeonggwa

Flavor, Aroma and Well-being
Sikhye & Sujeonggwa
[Sweet Rice Punch & Cinnamon Punch]

Korea's definitive drinks are *sikhye* (sweet rice punch) and *sujeonggwa* (cinnamon punch with dried persimmon). These beverages, made with medicinal herbs or grains to enhance the flavor and aroma and to boost energy, are usually served as dessert. *Hwache* (punch) is a classic fruit drink. Sour *omija-hwache* (five flavor berry punch) is enjoyed mainly in the winter. *Hwache* is prepared by soaking pieces of sweet fruit in honey water.

Sikhye, a Sweet Digestive Drink

Sikhye is a traditional dessert beverage made by fermenting rice in malt oil (*yeot-gireum*). Also known as sweet liquor (*gamju*), it is called *sikhye* if you drink it together with the grains and *gamju* when the liquor is separated out. *Sikhye's* essential ingredient is malt oil made from sprouted barley. Since malt oil is rich in amylase, a diastatic enzyme, *sikhye* has been traditionally offered as dessert drink after eating heavy meals on holidays. It was a favorite digestive tonic after overindulging during the days when other forms of digestive aids were not readily available.

Spicy and Sweet *Sujeonggwa*

Sujeonggwa is made by simmering ginger and cinnamon sticks, sweetening it with sugar or honey, and adding dried persimmons and pine nuts. Ginger and cinnamon are well-known for their medicinal qualities, but they also give off a spicy and aromatic flavor when boiled in water. *Sujeonggwa* is a cold drink normally consumed in winter, since the dried persimmons which are the principle ingredient are available only after late autumn. This drink is generally presented to guests who make courtesy calls on New Year's Day. The combined flavor of spicy cinnamon coupled with sweet dried persimmons and pine nuts is wonderful. In the old days, the whole family would sit together in the evenings and drink *sujeonggwa* with floating bits of ice.

Omija-hwache, a Ruby Colored Soft Drink
Clear red-colored *omija* (schisandra berry) tastes sweet, sour, bitter, salty, and spicy, all at the same time. This is where the name *omija* meaning "five flavor berry" came from. If you store well-dried *omija* berries in water, the color of the liquid turns into a translucent ruby red color. With the addition of small pieces of sweet fruit, it becomes *omija* punch. Sweet and crunchy pears are a common partner.

A Reflection of Poverty
Nurungji & Sungnyung
[Thin Layer of Scorched Rice & Browned Rice Tea]

When cooking rice there left a thin layer of scorched rice in the bottom, and it is called *nurungji*. *Nurungji* is a low-calorie food boasting crisp chewiness and sweetness. The more you chew it, the sweeter it tastes and makes you feel full. So it used to serve as a snack in the old days. *Sungnyung* is made when you add some water to this *nurungji* and boil it. In Korea natural water had a good quality, so *sungnyung* was more popularized than tea since the Joseon Dynasty.

Giving Sweet and Warm Tastes at the Same Time

In those old days when people cooked rice by burning firewood gathered in the mountains, they usually had a humble table with a bowl of rice, one or two kinds of kimchi, and a *jongji* (small dish) of soy sauce on it, but there was always delicious *sungnyung* at last. When you almost finish the meal, mother offers a bowl of boiled *nurungji*. The warm and delicious smell mixed within the rising steam from the bowl makes not only your nose but deep in your mind feel warm and cozy. In the past, mothers cooked rice by putting certain amount of water and rice in a cauldron, boiling it, and then simmering it enough until the water is gone. After they scooped deliciously cooked rice out of the pot, they also made *sungnyung* by adding some water to *nurungji* scorched in the bottom and boiling it again. *Nurungji* and *sungnyung* are very unique Korean food and beverage.

Nurungji was also used for medical purpose as well. In his book *Donguibogam* written in 1613, Heo Jun writes, "when food does not move smoothly through the throat or reach the stomach, or when you cannot eat food because of feeling nausea, it can be treated by *nurungji*. Boil a few-year-old *nurungji* and the river water together, and drink it any time of the day." Besides that, *nurungji* served as a snack for children who always wanted for sweets and an emergency food for those who had a trip to Seoul for a *gwageo,** went on a business far away, or traveled far.

It was not until the Bronze Age that the modern way of rice cooking started. Then since the Iron Age enabled people to use a caldron made of cast iron, rice cooking became common. *Sungnyung* was once a reflection of poverty. However *nurungji* and *sungnyung* are favored as a healthy food nowadays. Electric rice cookers have an extra function to make *nurungji* and you can find it as a packaged form in stores. For those who skip breakfast due to a busy schedule, a bowl of *sungnyung* with boiled *nurungji* fills and comforts your stomach.

---

* *Gwageo* were the national civil service examinations under the Goryeo and Joseon dynasties of Korea.

Gopdolsot

Gopdolsot is made by carving talc stone into the shape of a pot. This stone pot has low thermal conductivity, so it helps rice simmer evenly without the bottom getting burned. Hence the cooked rice tastes great and slow to get cold. In the old days people made *nurungji* by boiling a certain amount of rice and water in a cauldron and simmering it enough until the water disappears. They also made *sungnyung* by adding water to the scorched rice in the bottom of the pot and boiling it.

Liquor Rich in Lactobacilli and Dietary Fiber

Makgeolli

[Korean Rice Wine]

Makgeolli is a traditional Korean alcoholic beverage made from grains such as sweet rice, regular rice, barley and wheat, and malt. As *makgeolli* is made by fermenting grains, the lees (*suljigemi*) settle on the bottom. If you siphon off the clear liquor, it is called *cheongju*. *Makgeolli* is an undistilled spirit before separating out the *cheongju*, which is the origin of its name, meaning "not distilled."

Undistilled *Makgeolli*

Makgeolli is called by many names: *takju* meaning "cloudy liquor," *nongju* meaning "farmers liquor," *baekju* meaning "white liquor," and *dongdongju* or *bueuiju* meaning "wine with floating grains of rice." The fact that it has so many names reflects its popularity among common people. *Cheongju*, the clear liquid which rises above the rice sediment as the wine matures, is fifteen percent alcohol, while *makgeolli* is diluted to five to six percent.

Treasure Trove of Nutrients

Aside from the alcohol, the bulk of *makgeolli* is pure nutrition. Other than the 80 percent water and six to seven percent alcohol, *makgeolli* consists of two percent protein, 0.8 percent carbohydrates, 0.1 percent fat and ten percent dietary fiber, along with vitamins B and C, lactobacilli and yeast. It fully deserves its nickname: "a treasure trove of nutrients." One milliliter of undiluted *makgeolli* contains tens of millions of lactobacilli.

Makgeolli **Cocktail**
Even those unaccustomed to *makgeolli* can enjoy *makgeolli* cocktails. All sorts of different concoctions are available. Frozen *omija* (schisandra berry) juice can be ground with a spoon or puréed in a blender. With the addition of *makgeolli* to the sherbet, highly aromatic, sour red *omija-maekgeolli* can be enjoyed. Strawberry- or citrus-*makgeolli* can be made in the same manner. Other variations made with ginseng and honey or red ginseng concentrates offer exceptional flavor and aroma and also are believed to provide health benefits.

Makgeolli's **Dietary Fiber**
A bowl of *makgeolli* contains dietary fiber ranging from 100 to as much as 1,000 times the amount found in so-called "fiber beverages." Dietary fiber promotes digestion, and helps prevent constipation and heart disease.

INDEX

Photo Credit

- Korean Food Promotion Institute (http://www.hansik.or.kr)
- Page 54: Foodad (http://www.foodad.co.kr)
- Page 56: Institute of Traditional Korean Food (http://www.kfr.or.kr)
- Page 234: Funshop (http://raksik.funshop.co.kr)